NanoCAD 5.0 Basics Tutorial

Tutorial Books

Contents

Tutorial 1: Creating the Floor Plan

In this example, you will learn to create an architectural drawing.

Creating Outer Walls

- Double-click on the **NanoCAD en 5.0** icon on your desktop.
- Click the **Get Started** icon on the **NanoCAD 5.0** pop up window; a new document is created.

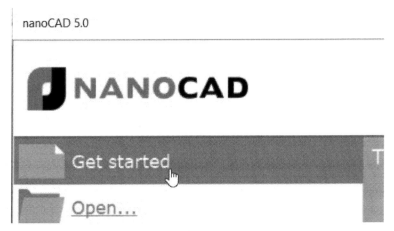

The components of the NanoCAD user interface are shown in the figure given next:

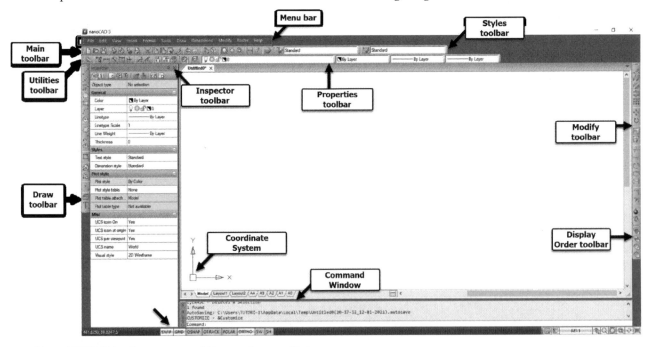

- Type **UNITS** in the command line and press Enter.

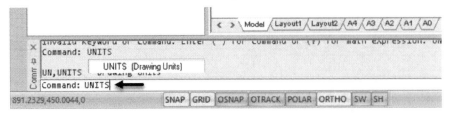

- On the **Drawing Units** dialog, select **Type > Architectural** from the **Length** section. Next, select **Precision**

> 0-0 1/16.

- Select **Inches** from the **Units to scale inserted content** drop-down in the **Insertion Scale** section. Next, click **OK**.

- Type LIMITS in the command line and press Enter.

- Press Enter to accept 0, 0 as the lower limit.

- Type **100', 80'** in the command line, and press Enter. The program sets the upper limit of the drawing.

- Make sure that the **Grid** icon is turned OFF on the status bar.

- On the menu bar, click **View > Zoom > Zoom Extents**.

- On the Status bar, turn ON the **Ortho** icon.

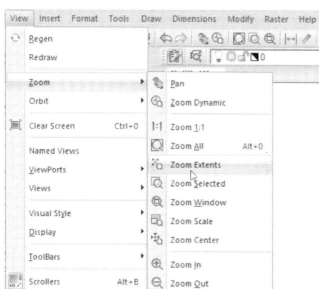
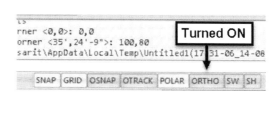

- On the Draw toolbar, click the **Line by Points** icon, and then select an arbitrary point. It defines the start point of the line.

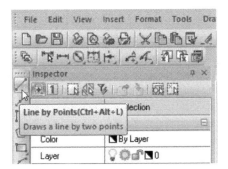

- Move the pointer toward the right horizontally and type **@412<0** in the command line – press Enter.

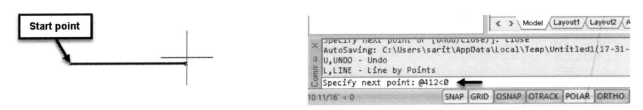

- In the command line, type **@338<90** and press Enter.
- Move the pointer onto the starting point of the drawing, and then move it upwards. You will notice that a dotted line appears.

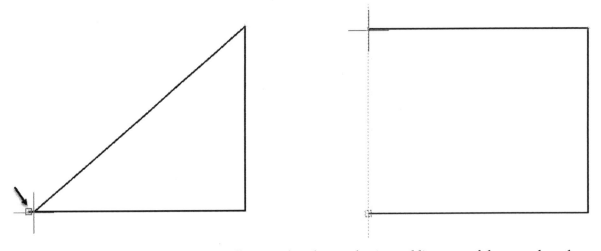

- Click to create a horizontal line. You will notice that the two horizontal lines are of the same length.
- Click the right mouse button and select **Close**.

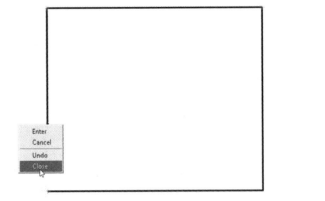

- On the **Modify** Toolbar, click the **Offset Object** icon. Next, type-in **6** in the command line and press Enter.

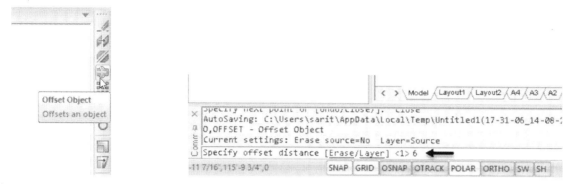

- Select the left vertical line of the drawing.
- Move the pointer inside the drawing and click to create an offset line.
- Likewise, offset the other lines, as shown below.

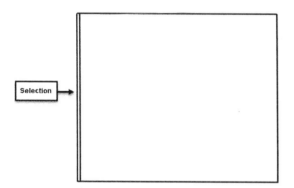

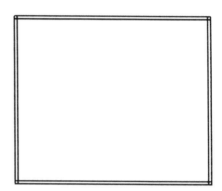

- On the menu bar, click **View > Zoom > Zoom Window**.
- Create a window on the top left corner of the drawing. The corner portion will be zoomed in.

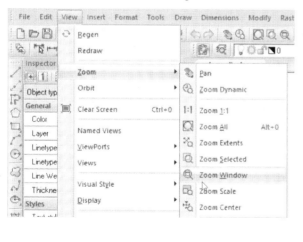

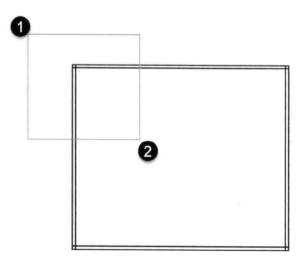

- On the Modify Toolbar, click the **Fillet** icon; the Fillet dialog appears on the screen.
- Type **0** in the **Radius** box and click **OK**.

- Select the inner offset lines, as shown below. Next, press ESC.

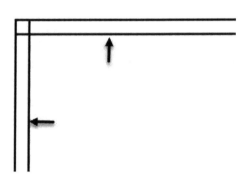
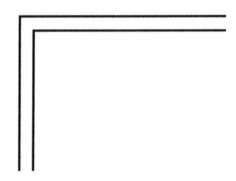

- On the **View** tab > **Zoom** > **Zoom Extents** on the menu bar.

- On the menu bar, click **Home** > **Modify** > **Fillet**. Select the inner offset lines, as shown below.

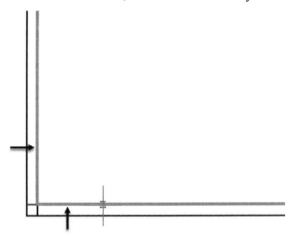

- Likewise, fillet the other inner corners, as shown.

- Click **File > Save** on the Menu bar. Next, type **Tutorial_1** in the **File name** box and click Save.

- Make sure that you save the drawing after each section.

Creating Inner Walls

- On the **Modify** toolbar, click the **Offset Object** icon. Next, type **130** in the command line and press Enter.

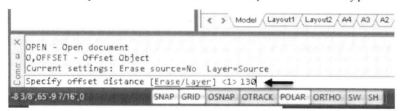

- Select the inner line of the right sidewall. Next, move the pointer toward the left and click.

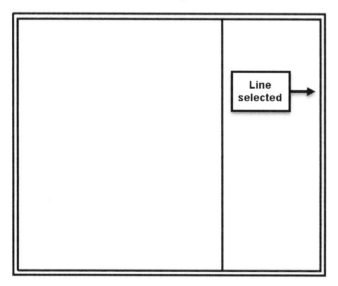

- Click the **Exit** option on the Command Window.

- Activate the **Offset Object** command. Next, type **4** in the Command line and press Enter.

- Select the new offset line and move the pointer toward the left. Next, click to create another offset line and press **Esc**.

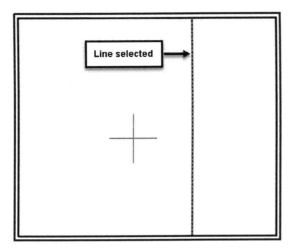
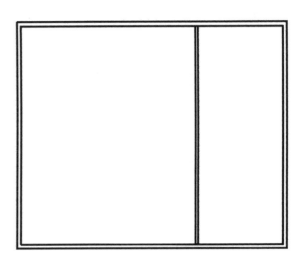

- Activate the **Offset Object** command and type **118**. Press Enter.
- Select the line, as shown in the figure. Next, move the pointer towards the left and click to create the offset line.

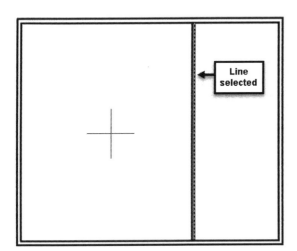
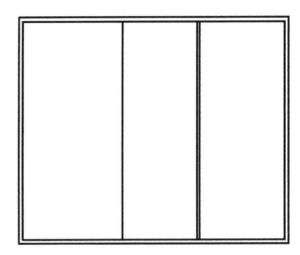

- Likewise, create another offset line with offset distance **122**, as shown below.

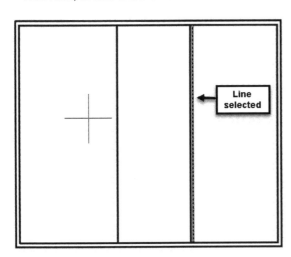
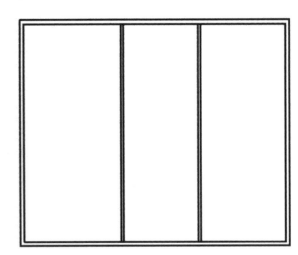

- Likewise, create horizontal offset lines, as shown below.

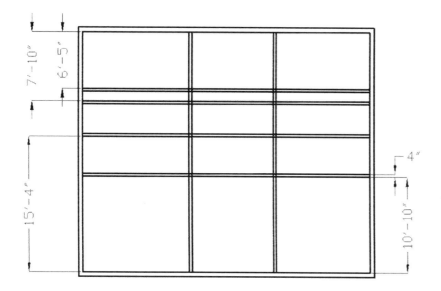

- On the menu bar, click **Modify > Trim Vectors** (or) click the **Trim Vectors by Edge** icon on the **Modify Toolbar.**

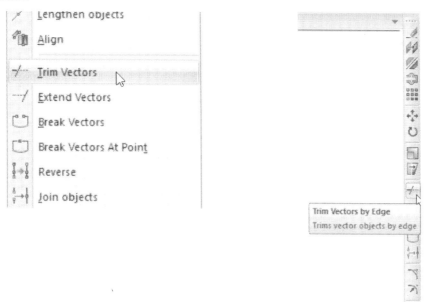

- Press Enter to select all the elements of the drawing.
- Select the **Crossing** option on the Command window, as shown.

```
TR,TRIM - Trim vectors by Edge
Current settings: Projection="None", Edge="No extend"
20 found
Select objects (enter -- select all) or [?/]:
Select object to trim (+shift -- to extend) or [?/Fence/Crossing/Project/Edge/eRase/Back]:
9-6 15/16",65'-10 5/8",0    SNAP  GRID  OSNAP  OTRACK  POLAR  ORTHO  SW  SH
```

- Press and hold the left mouse button and drag a selection box across the horizontal lines, as shown below.

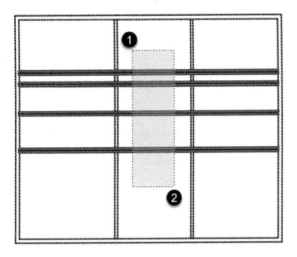 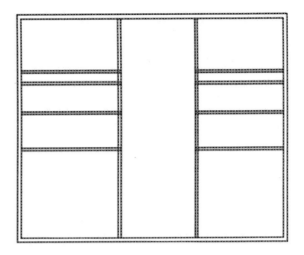

- Likewise, trim other entities using the Crossing option on the command window, as shown below.

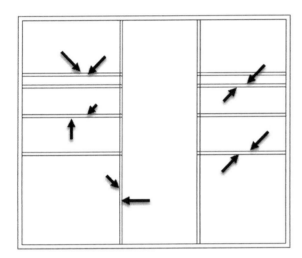 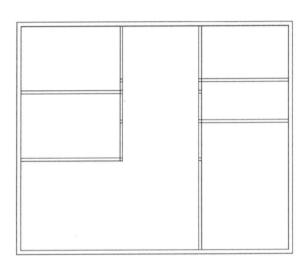

- Make sure that the **Trim Vectors** command is active.
- On the command window, click the **Crossing** option.
- Click and drag a selection box across the elements, as shown. Next, press **Esc** to exit the command.

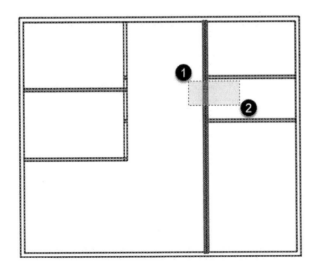 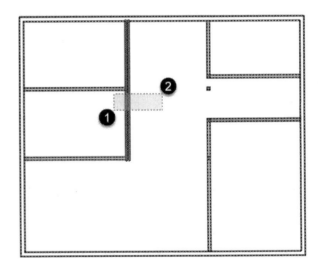

- Zoom to the top portion of the drawing by placing the pointer in the top portion and rotating the mouse scroll in the forward direction.
- On the menu bar, click **Modify > Trim Vectors**. Next, press ENTER to select all the elements as cutting edges.
- Select the portion of the horizontal line between the inner walls' lines by using the selection box.

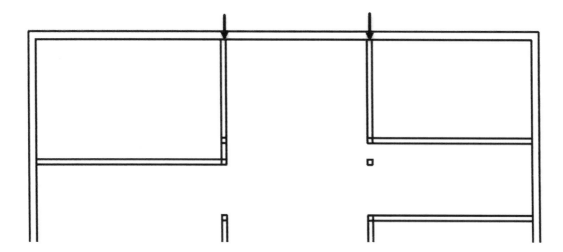

The selected portions will be trimmed.

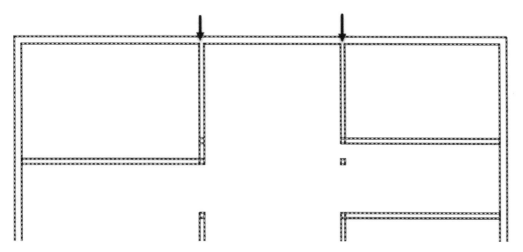

- Press and hold the mouse scroll wheel and drag downwards until the lower portion of the drawing is visible.
- Trim the unwanted portion, as shown below.

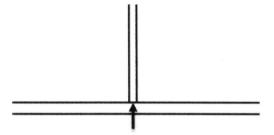

- Trim the unwanted portions, as shown below. Also, trim the unwanted portions at the corners.

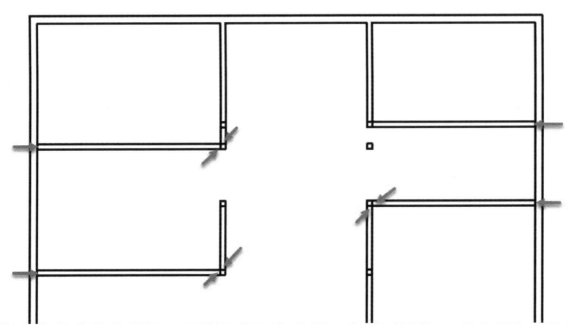

- Make sure that the **Trim Vectors** command is active. Next, select the **eRase** option on the Command window.

- Select the unwanted elements, as shown. Next, press ENTER.

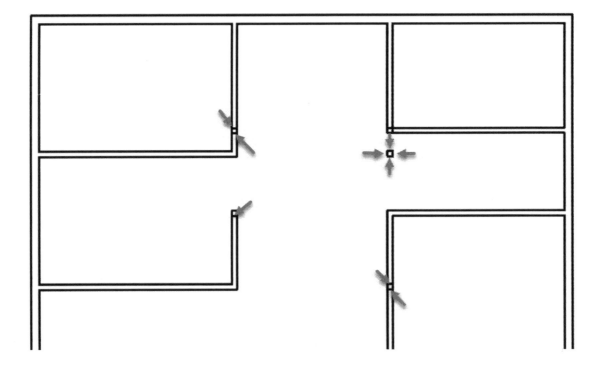

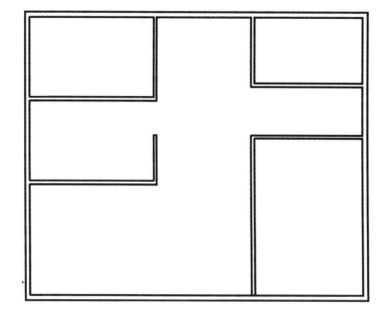

Creating Openings and Doors

- Activate the **Line by Points** command and select the corner of the inner wall, as shown below.

- Move the pointer downward and select the other corner point.

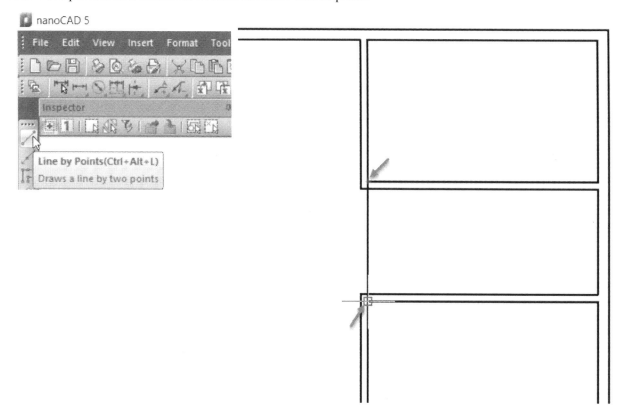

- Press **Esc** and select the new line.

- Select the middle point of the new line and move the pointer toward the right.

- Type-in **6** and press Enter.

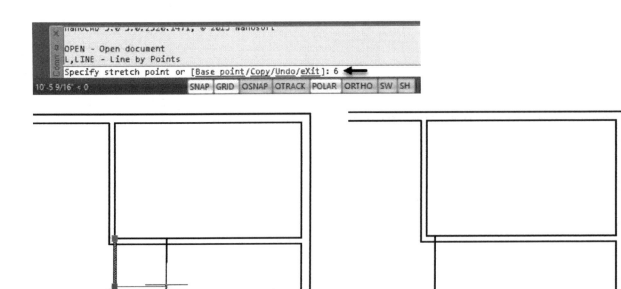

- On the menu bar, click **Modify > Offset** command. Type **32** as the offset distance, and then press ENTER.

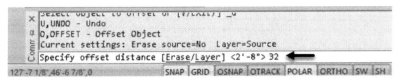

- Select the new line and move the pointer towards the right, and then click.

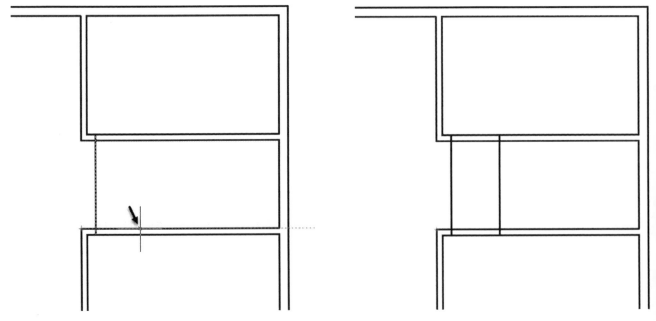

- On the Command Window, click the **Exit** option.

- On the menu bar, click **Modify >Trim Vectors**.

- Press Enter to select all the elements as the boundary edges.

- Click the **Crossing** option on the Command Window.

```
Current settings: Projection="None", Edge="No extend"
11 found
Select objects (enter -- select all) or [?/]:
Select object to trim (+shift -- to extend) or [?/Fence/Crossing/Project/Edge/eRase/Back]:
-1 5/8",46'-9",0          SNAP  GRID  OSNAP  OTRACK  POLAR  ORTH  SW  SH
```

- Click and drag a selection box across the unwanted portions, as shown below.

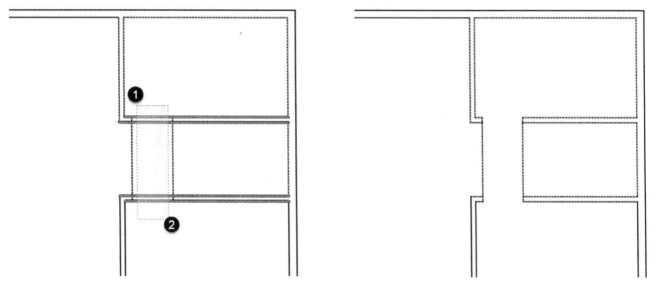

- Make sure that the **Trim Vectors** command is active. Next, click the **Crossing** option on the Command window.

- Click and drag a selection box across the unwanted portions, as shown below.

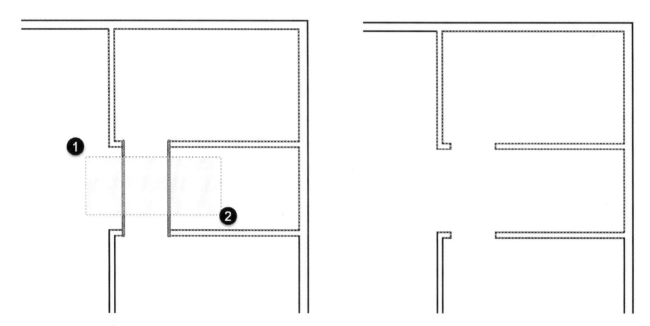

- Activate the **Line by Points** command and create the lines, as shown below.
- Offset the newly created lines. The offset distances are given in the figure below.

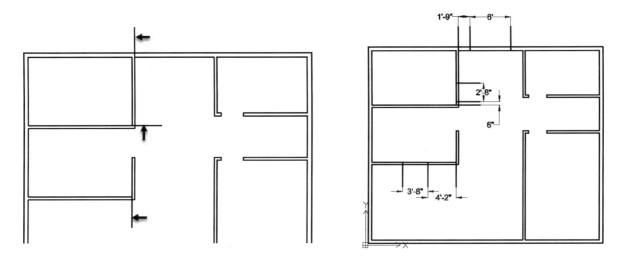

- On the menu bar, click **Modify > Trim Vectors** to trim the unwanted portions.

- Press Enter to select all the elements as the boundary edges.

- Select the **Crossing** option to trim the lines and draw a selection box, as shown.

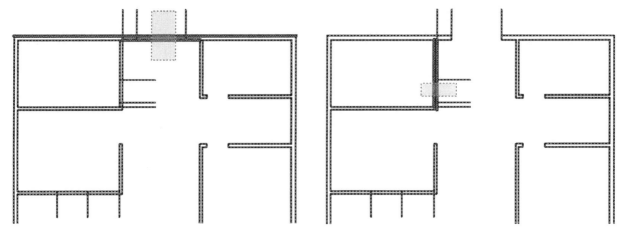

- Likewise, select the **Crossing** option and draw a selection box for the rest of the lines, as shown.

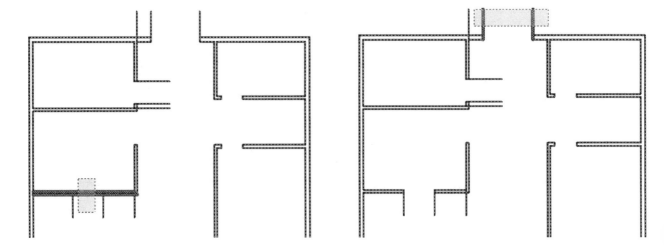

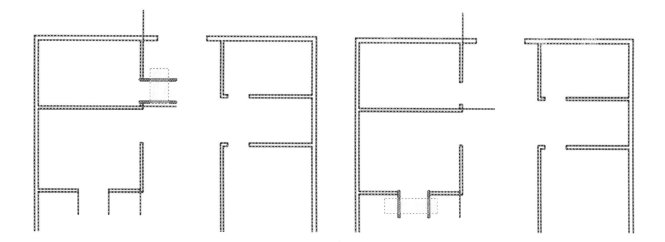

- Press **Esc** on the Keyboard.

- Select the remaining unwanted lines and press DELETE.

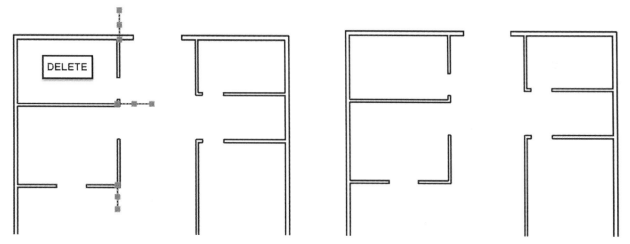

- On the menu bar, click **Draw > Rectangle by > Two Points**. Next, select the endpoint of the opening, as shown below.

- Right click and select **Dimensions** from the shortcut menu.

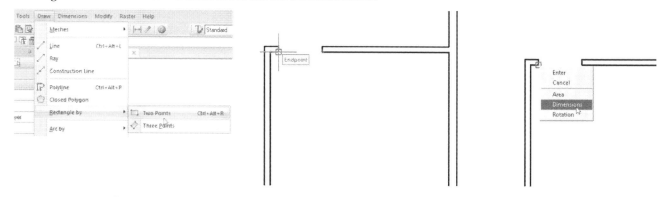

- Type-in **1** and press Enter. It defines the length of the rectangle.

- Type-in **32** and press Enter. It defines the width of the rectangle.

- Move the pointer downward and click.

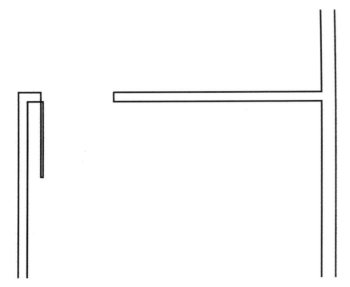

Now, you need to create the door swing.

- On the menu bar, click **Draw > Arc by > Center, Start, Angle**.
- Select the top left corner of the rectangle to define the center of the arc.
- Select the bottom left corner of the rectangle to define the starting point of the arc.
- Select the corner point of the opening, as shown.
- Move the pointer upward and click.

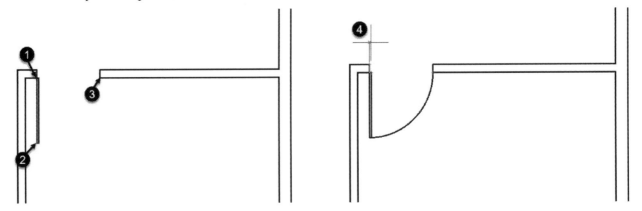

- Select the door and door swing.
- On the menu bar, click **Modify > Copy**. Next, select the corner point of the rectangle as the base point.

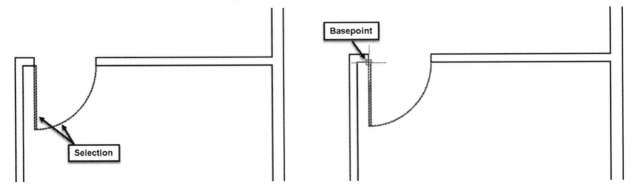

- Select the corner points of openings, as shown below.

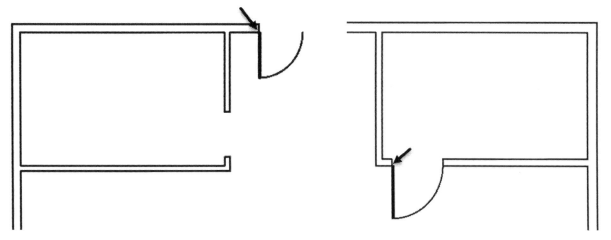

- Press Esc to deactivate the **Copy** command.

- Click the right mouse button on the **OSNAP** icon on the status bar. Next, select **Drafting Settings** from the menu.

- On the **Drafting Settings**, click the **Object Snap** tab and select the **Midpoint** option

- Next, click **OK** on the dialog.

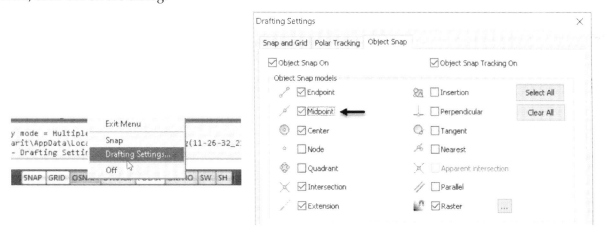

- On the menu bar, click **Modify > Mirror**, and then select the door and swing of the bathroom, as shown. Press Enter to accept the selection.

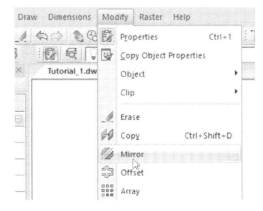

- Define the mirror line by selecting the points, as shown below.

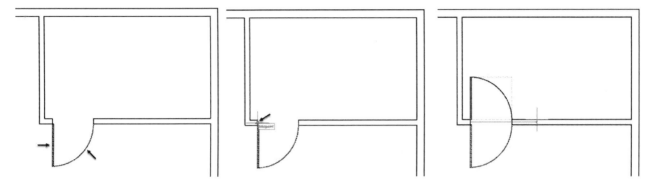

- Select **Yes** to delete the original object.

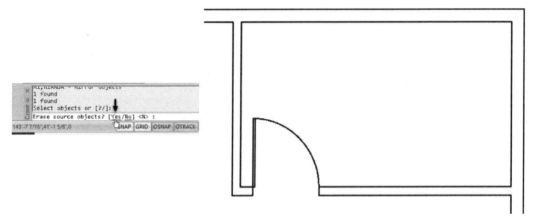

- Click the **Scale** icon on the **Modify** toolbar, and then select the door & swing at the main entrance — press Enter.
- Select the base point, as shown below.

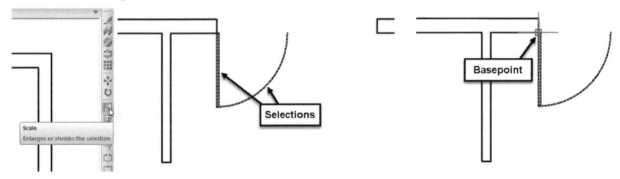

- Right click and select the **Reference Length** option from the shortcut menu.
- Select the two endpoints, as shown below. It defines the reference length of the objects. Now, you need to define the length up to which you want to scale the objects.
- Type-in **36** and press Enter. The objects will be scaled.

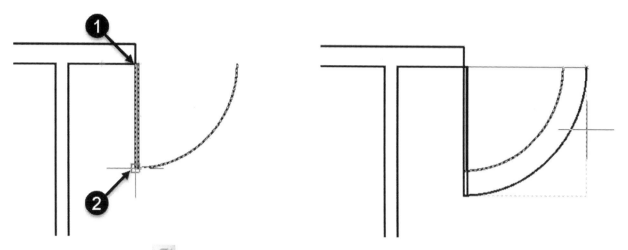

- Activate the **Mirror** 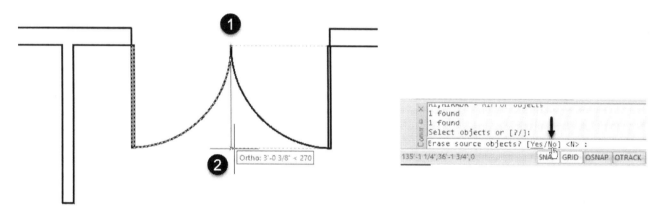 command and select the door & swing at the entrance. Press Enter to accept the selection.
- Define the mirror line by selecting the points, as shown below.
- Select **No** to keep the original object.

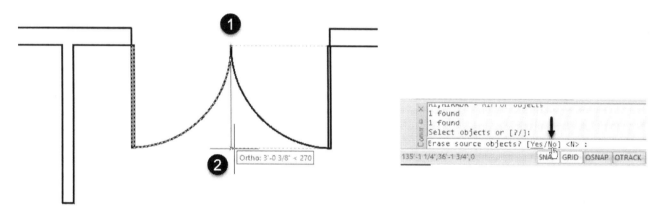

- Copy the door & swing of the bathroom and place it at the opening, as shown below.
- Press Esc.

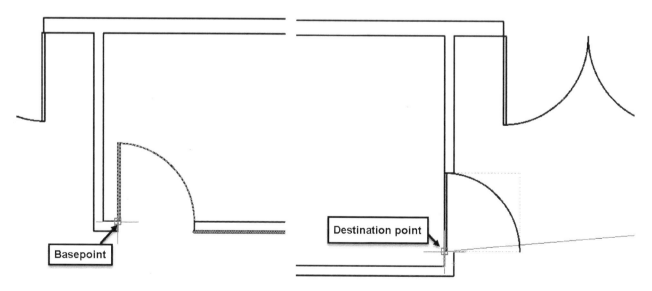

- On the menu bar, click **Modify > Rotate**, and then select the copied object. Next, press Enter.

- Select the base point, as shown. Next, move the pointer vertically upward, and then click.

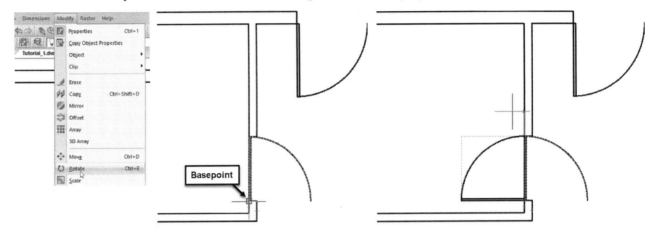

- Create an opening on the rear side of the plan, as shown below.

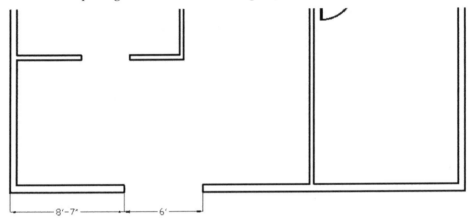

Now, you will create a sliding door in the opening.

- Activate the **Rectangle by Two Points** ▢ command and select the opening's corner point, as shown below.

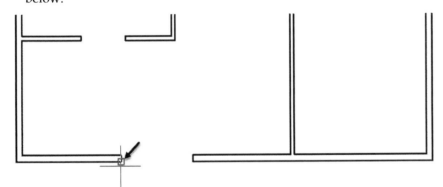

- Right click and select the **Dimensions** option. Next, type 37 and press ENTER to define the length.
- Type 2 and press ENTER to define the width of the rectangle.
- Move the pointer upward and click to create the rectangle.

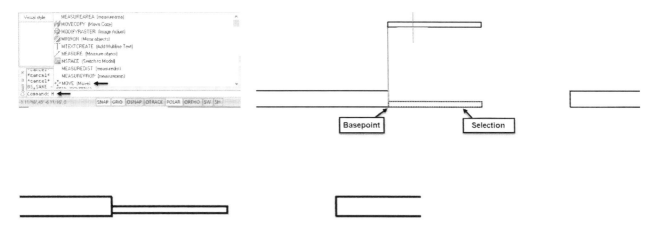

- Type **M** in the command line and press Enter. Select the rectangle, and then press Enter.
- Select its lower-left corner point to define the base point. Move the pointer upward and type-in 1 in the command line, and then press Enter.

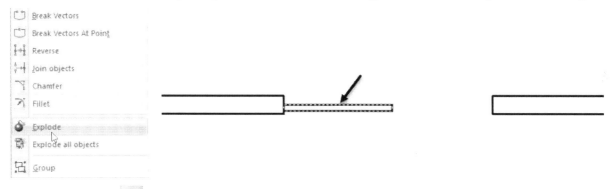

- On the menu bar, click **Modify > Explode**, and select the rectangle. Press Enter to explode the rectangle.

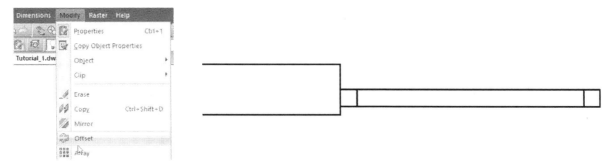

- Activate the **Offset** command and specify 2 as the offset distance.
- Offset the left and right vertical lines of the rectangle. Press **Esc** to deactivate the **Offset** command.

- Activate the **Line** command and select the midpoints of the offset lines. It creates a line connecting the offset lines. It creates one part of the sliding door.

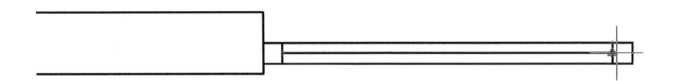

- Press **Esc** to deactivate the **Line** command.

- Type-in **CO** and press Enter. Next, drag a selection window covering all the elements of the sliding door. Press Enter.

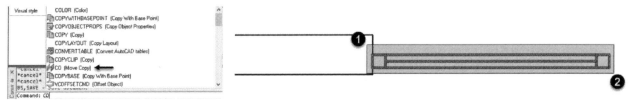

- Select the lower-left corner of the sliding door as the base point.

- Move the pointer and select the endpoint of the offset line, as shown.

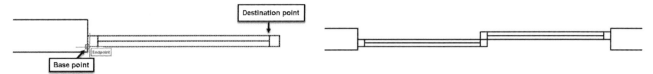

- Press **Esc** to deactivate the **Copy** command.

Now, you need to draw thresholds on the door openings.

- Zoom to the front door area using the **Zoom Window** tool.

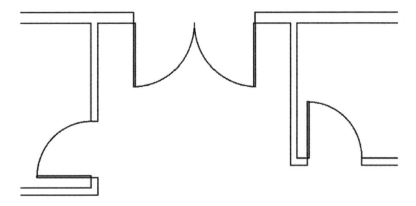

- On the menu bar, click **Draw > Rectangle by > Three Points**. Select the left corner point of the door opening.

- Move the pointer toward the right and select the right corner point of the door opening.

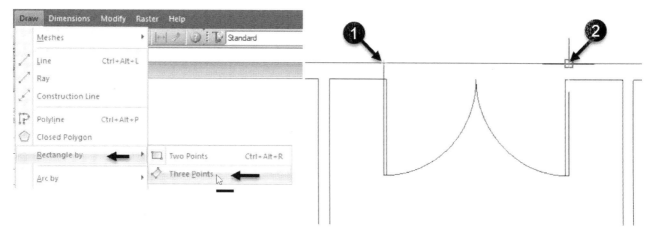

- Move the pointer upward and type 2. Next, press ENTER to create a rectangle.

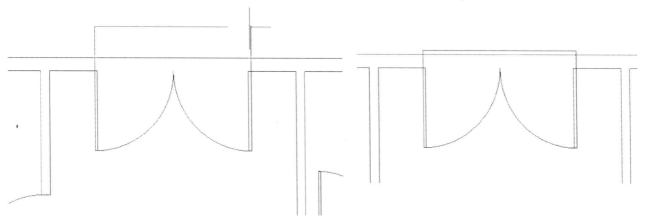

- Place the pointer on the double-door and roll the scroll wheel upwards.
- Select the select newly created rectangle.
- Select the Midpoint grip of the rectangle's left vertical edge and move the pointer toward the left.

- Type 3 and press ENTER.

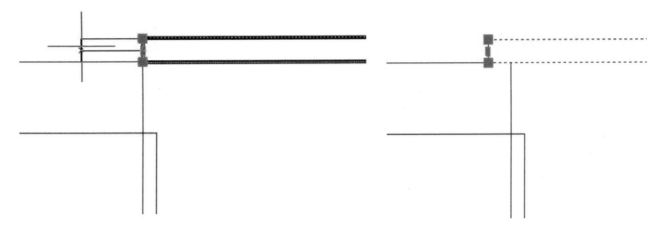

- Select the Midpoint grip of the right vertical edge of the rectangle and move the pointer toward the right.

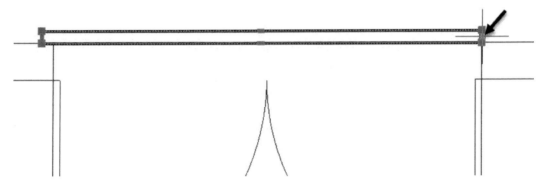

- Type 3 and press ENTER.

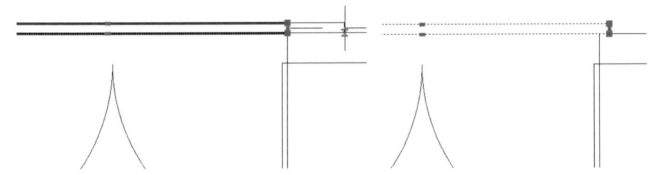

- Select the rectangle and click **Modify > Explode** on the menu bar.

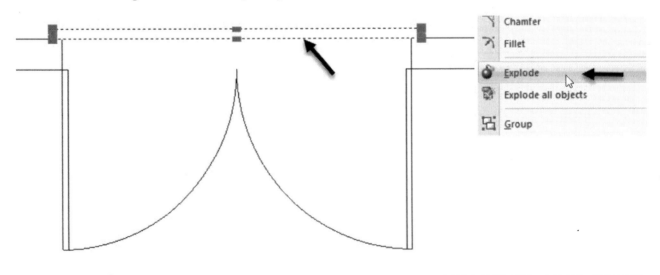

- Select the bottom horizontal line of the rectangle and press DELETE.

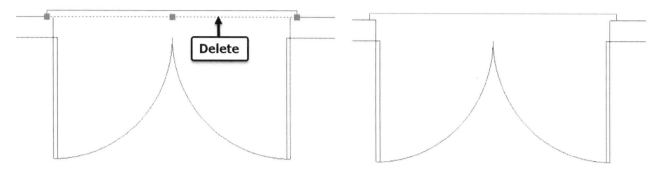

- Likewise, create a threshold on the sliding glass door.

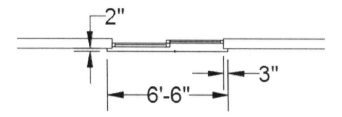

Creating Kitchen Fixtures

- Zoom to the kitchen area by using the **Zoom Window** tool.

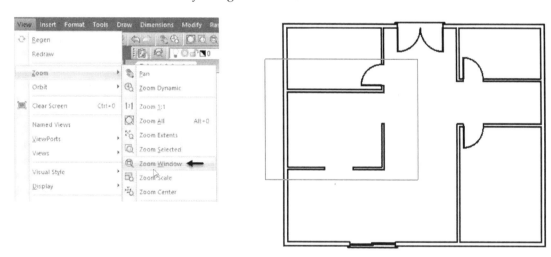

- Activate the **Offset Object** command and specify **26** as the offset distance. Next, offset the lines shown below.

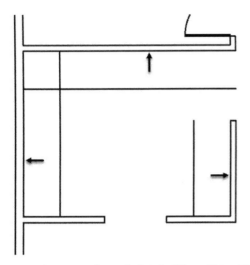

- On the menu bar, click **Modify > Trim Vectors**. Next, press ENTER to select all the elements.

- Select the unwanted portions, as shown.

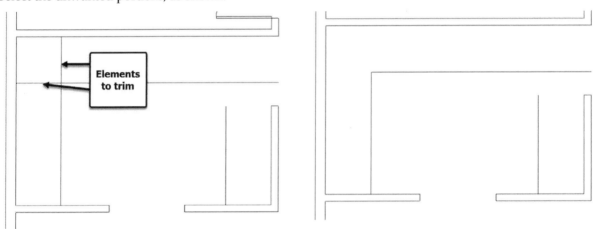

- Create another offset line at **54** distance, and then trim the unwanted elements.

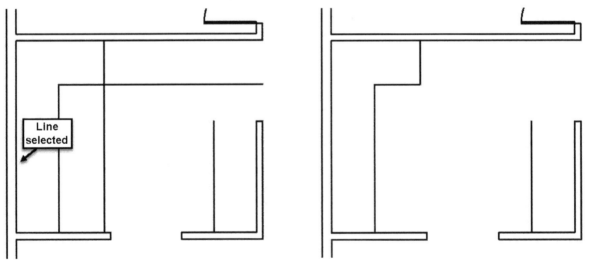

- Create another line, as shown below.

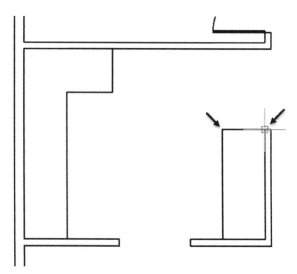

Now, you have finished drawing the counters. You need to draw a refrigerator, stove and sink.

- On the menu bar, click **Draw > Rectangle by > Two Points**.
- Select the corner point of the counter. Next, right-click and select the **Dimensions** option.
- Type **28** and press ENTER to define the horizontal dimension.
- Type **28** and press ENTER to define the vertical dimension.
- Move the pointer towards the right and click to create the rectangle.

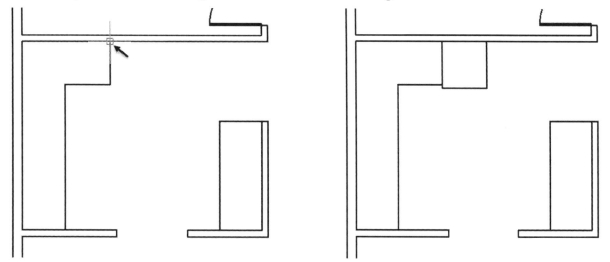

- Select the rectangle and click **Modify > Move** on the menu bar.
- Select the top left corner of the rectangle. Next, move the pointer toward the right and type **2**. Press ENTER to move the rectangle.
- Likewise, move the rectangle **2** inches and downwards.

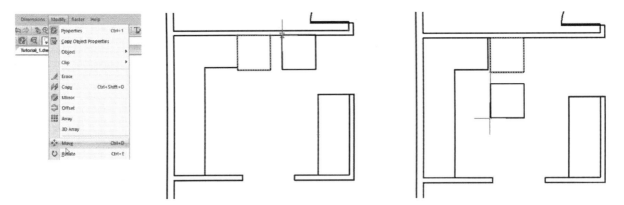

- Create the outline of the stove using the **Offset Object** and **Trim Vector** commands.

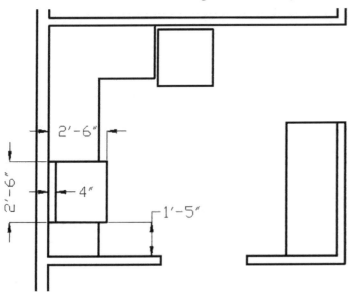

Now, you need to create the sink.

- Use the **Offset Object** command and create offset lines, as shown below.

- Trim the unwanted elements, as shown below.

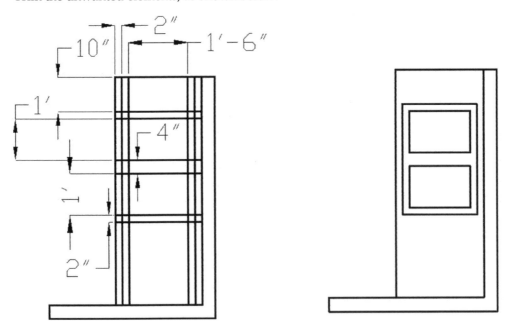

- On the menu bar, click **Modify > Fillet**. The **Fillet** dialog appears on the screen.

- Type **2** in the radius box and click **OK**. Next, select the horizontal and vertical lines forming a corner, as shown.

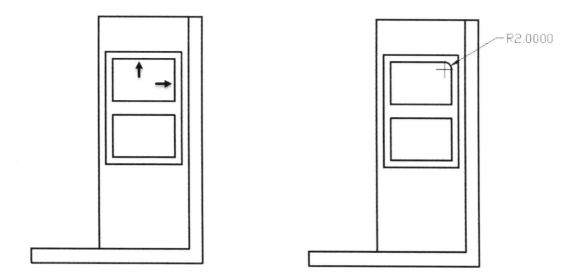

- Likewise, fillet the remaining corners with a fillet radius of 2 and 4, respectively.

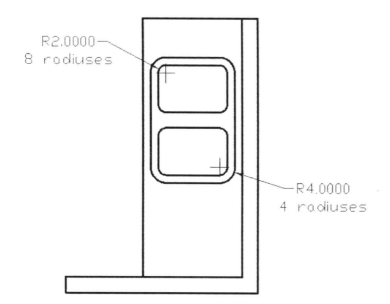

- On the menu bar, click **Draw > Construction Line**. Next, select the **Hor** option from the command line.

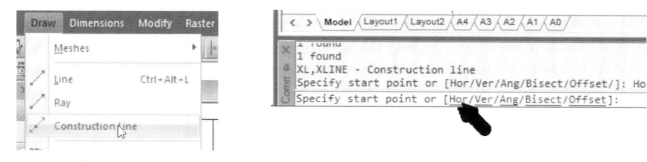

- Select the midpoint of the vertical line, as shown.

- Likewise, create another horizontal construction line by selecting the midpoint of the vertical line, as shown.

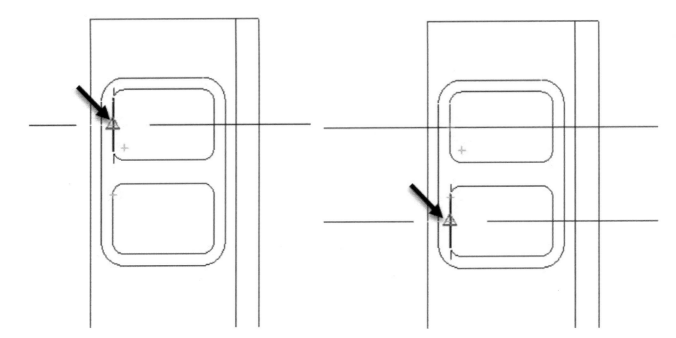

- Press ENTER twice to deactivate the **Construction Line** command and then activate it again.
- Select the **Ver** option from the command line.
- Select the midpoint of the horizontal line, as shown.
- Press **Esc** to deactivate the **Construction Line** command.

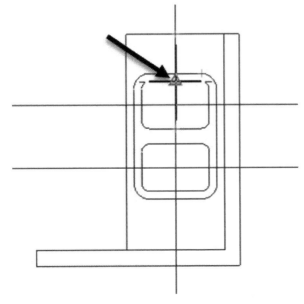

- On the menu bar, click **Draw > Circle > Center Radius**.

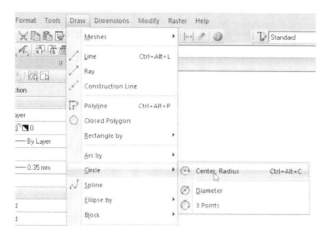

- Select the intersection point of the two construction lines, as shown.

- Select the **Diameter** option from the command line.

- Move the pointer outward, and then type **4**. Next, press ENTER.

- Press ENTER and select the intersection point of the construction lines.

- Select the **Diameter** option from the command line. Next, move the pointer outward, type **6**, and press ENTER.

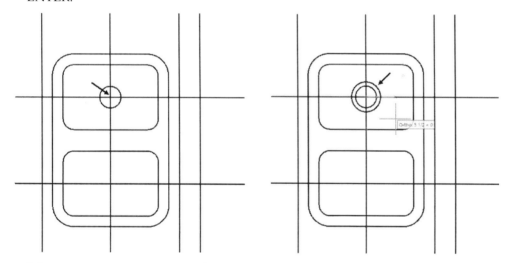

- Likewise, create two more circles, as shown. Next, delete the construction lines.

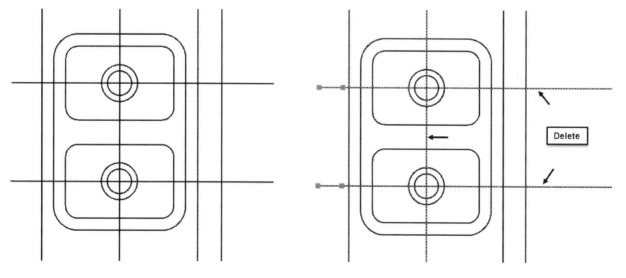

Creating Bathroom Fixtures

- Zoom into the bathroom area and create offset lines, as shown below.

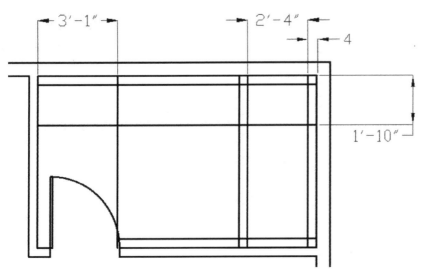

- Trim the unwanted elements, as shown below.
- Fillet the corners, as shown below. The fillet radius is **4**.

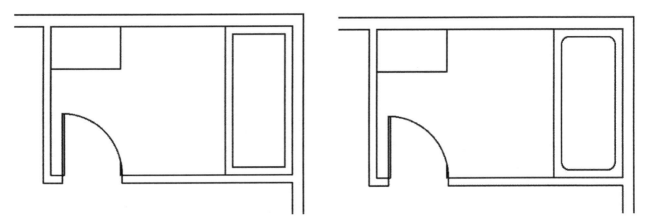

- Create two construction lines, as shown.

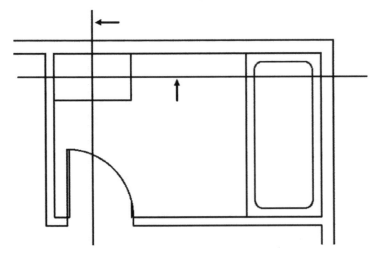

- On the menu bar, click **Draw > Ellipse by > Center and Radiuses**.
- Select the intersection point of the construction lines, as shown.

- Move the pointer toward the right and type in **10**, and then press Enter. It defines the major radius of the ellipse.

- Move the pointer downward and type in **5**, and then press Enter. It defines the minor radius of the ellipse.

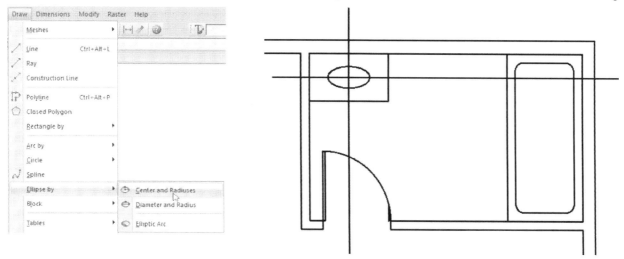

- Likewise, create another ellipse of **11** major radius and **7** minor radius.

- Delete the construction lines.

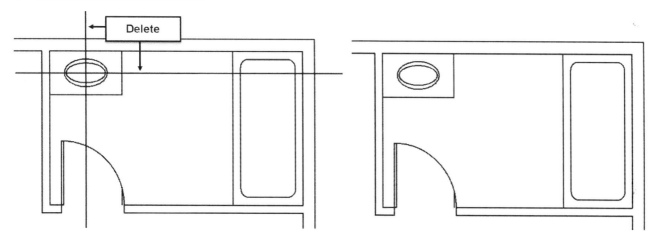

- Select the outer ellipse, and then click on its center point.

- Move the pointer up and type-in **1**, and then press Enter. The outer ellipse moves up.

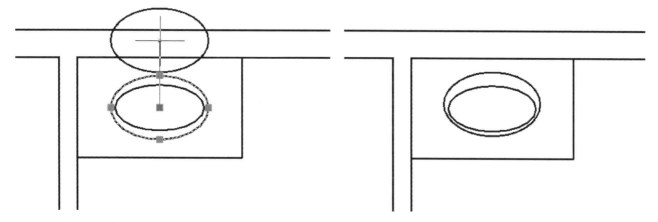

- On the menu bar, click **Draw > Rectangle by > Three Points**.

- Select the top-right corner of the washbasin. Next, move the pointer vertically downward.

- Type **9** and press ENTER. Next, move the pointer horizontally toward the right.
- Type **22** and press ENTER.

- Move the rectangle up to **19.5** rightwards and **1** downwards.

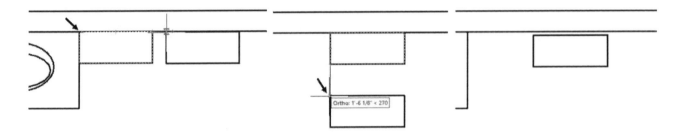

- On the menu bar, click **Draw > Ellipse by > Diameter and Radius**.
- Select the midpoint of the lower horizontal line of the rectangle.
- Move the pointer downward and type in **18**, and then press Enter.
- Move the pointer towards the right and type-in **6** as the minor axis, and press Enter.

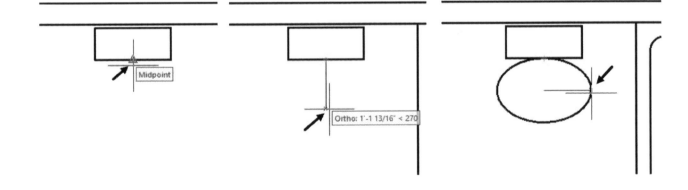

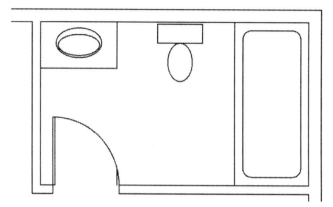

Adding Furniture using Blocks

- On the menu bar, click **Draw > Rectangle by > Two Points**.

- Click in the empty space to specify the first corner of the rectangle.

- Right-click and select **Dimensions** from the shortcut menu.

- Type **72** as the length of the rectangle and press ENTER.

- Type **36** as the width of the rectangle and press ENTER. Next, click to create the rectangle.

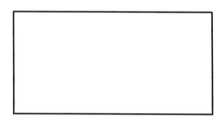

- On the menu bar, click **Draw > Rectangle by > Two Points**.

- Click in the empty space to specify the first corner of the rectangle.

- Select the **Dimensions** option from the command line.

- Type **18** as the length of the rectangle and press ENTER.

- Type **18** as the width of the rectangle and press ENTER. Click to create the rectangle.

- On the menu bar, click **Modify > Move**. Next, select the second rectangle and press ENTER.

- Select the midpoint of the right vertical line as a Basepoint, as shown.

- Move the pointer towards the right and select the midpoint of the first rectangle's left vertical line, as shown.

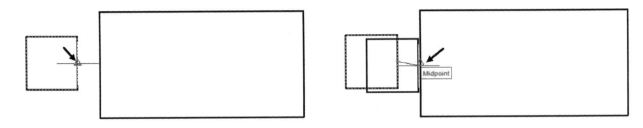

- Press Enter to activate the **Move** command. Next, select the second rectangle and press Enter.
- Select the midpoint of the vertical line as a Basepoint, as shown.
- Move the pointer horizontally towards the left and type **1**. Press Enter.

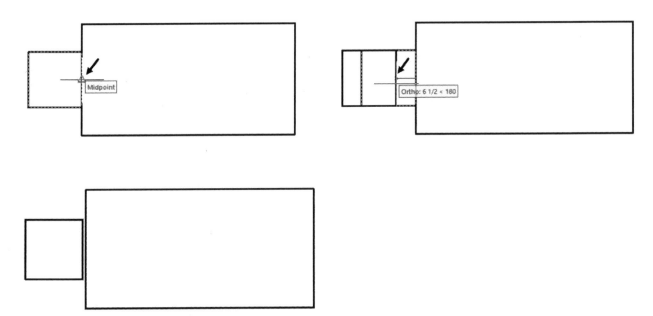

- Click the **Chamfer** icon on the **Modify** toolbar; the **Chamfer** dialog appears on the screen.
- On the dialog, select the **Two Lengths** icon, as shown. Type **2** in the **Length 1** and type **18** in the **Length 2** boxes.
- Deactivate the **Measure Chamfer** icon on the **Chamfer** dialog. Next, click **OK** on the dialog.

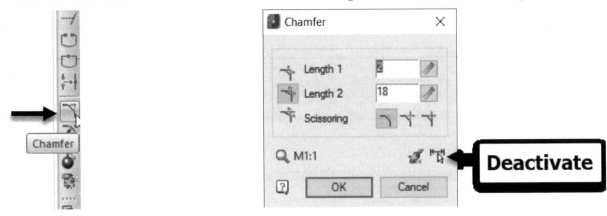

- Select the left vertical and horizontal bottom edges of the rectangle, as shown.
- Select the left vertical and top horizontal edges of the rectangle. Next, press ESC to deactivate the

command.

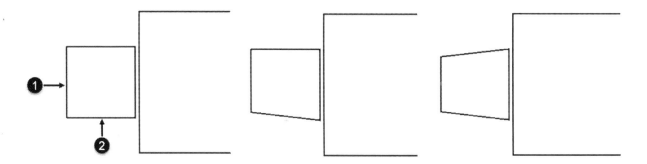

- Select the chamfered rectangle and click **Modify > Mirror** ![icon] on the menu bar.
- Select the midpoint of the lower horizontal edge of the large rectangle.
- Move the pointer vertically upward and click to define the mirror line.
- Next, select the **No** option on the Command line to keep the original object.

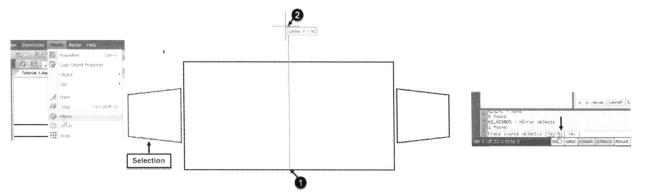

- Select the chamfered rectangle on the left side.
- Click **Modify > Rotate** on the menu bar.
- Select the midpoint of the top horizontal edge of the large rectangle.

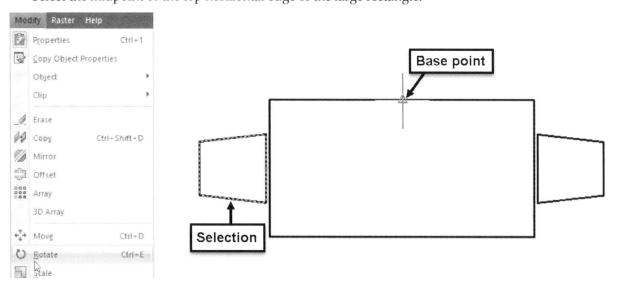

- Select the **Copy** option from the Command Line.

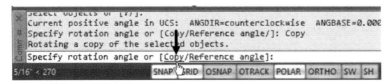

- Move the pointer vertically upward and click to copy the selected entity.

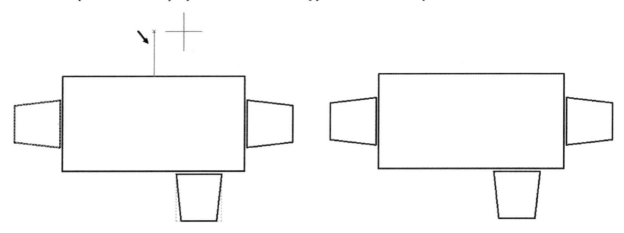

- Mirror the rotated rectangle, as shown.

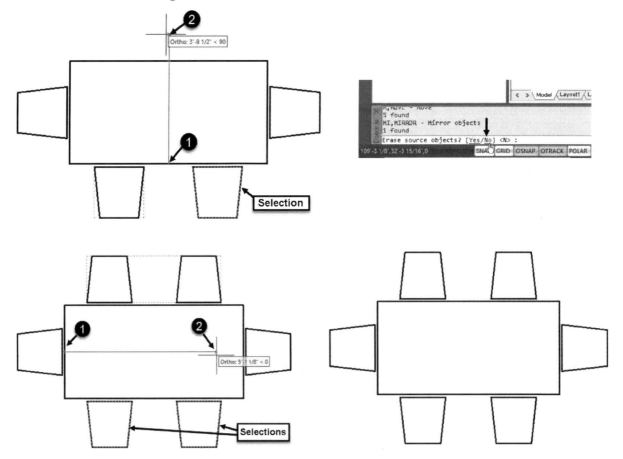

- On the menu bar, click **Draw > Rectangle by > Two Points**.

- Click in the empty space. Next, right click and select **Dimensions**.

- Type **80** as the length of the rectangle and press ENTER.

- Type **62** as the width of the rectangle and press ENTER. Click to create the rectangle.

- Press ENTER and select the midpoint of the right vertical edge of the rectangle. Next, right click and select **Dimensions**.
- Type **15** as the length of the rectangle and press ENTER.
- Type **20** as the width of the rectangle and press ENTER.
- Move the pointer upwards. Next, move the pointer leftwards and click to create another rectangle, as shown.

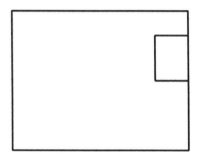

- Select the newly created rectangle.
- Click **Modify > Move** on the menu bar.
- Click on the lower right corner of the rectangle as a Basepoint.
- Move the pointer towards the left and type **2** in the command line. Press Enter.

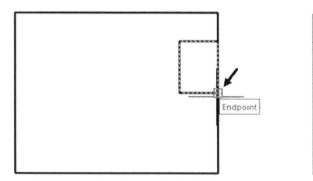 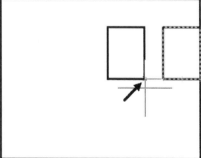

- Likewise, move the rectangle upwards by **2** inches, as shown.

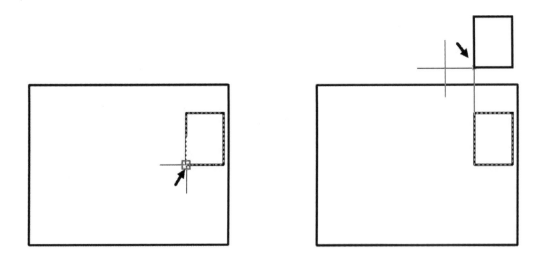

- Create a mirrored copy of the rectangle, as shown.

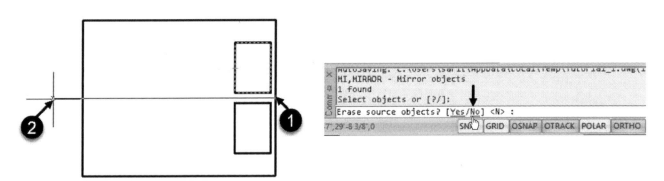

- Select the large rectangle of the bed and click **Explode selected entities** on the **Modify** Toolbar.

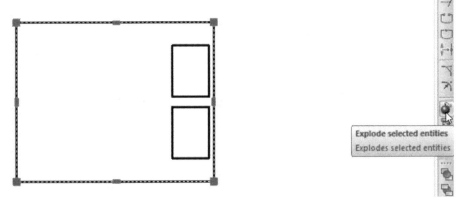

- Select the right vertical line of the exploded rectangle and click **Modify > Offset** on the menu bar.

- Type **14** in the command line and press ENTER. Next, move the pointer toward the left and click.

- Select the **Exit** command on the command line.

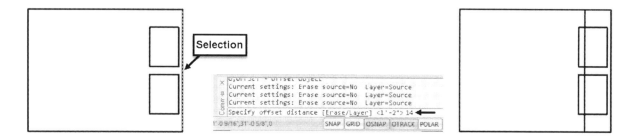

- Press ENTER to activate the **Offset** command. Type **4** in the command line and press ENTER.
- Select the offset line and move the pointer toward the left. Next, click to create another offset line.

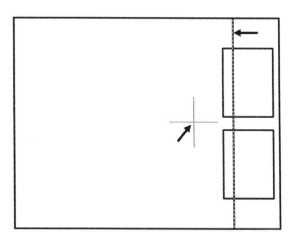 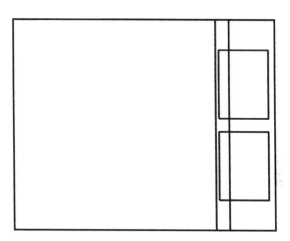

- Click **Draw** > **Rectangle by** > **Two Points** on the menu bar.
- Select the lower endpoint of the first offset line. Next, right-click and select **Dimensions**.
- Type **15** and press ENTER to define the length of the rectangle.
- Type **15** and press ENTER to define the width of the rectangle.
- Click inside the large rectangle to create another rectangle.

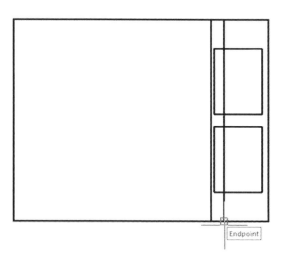 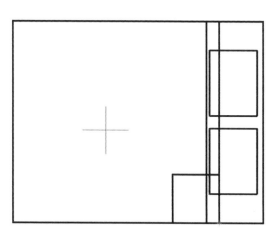

- On the menu bar, click **Draw** > **Line**. Next, select the top-right and bottom-left corners of the newly created rectangle.

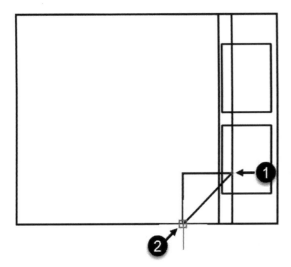

- Press **Esc** to deactivate the **Line** command.
- Select the newly created rectangle and click **Explode selected entities** on the **Modify** Toolbar.

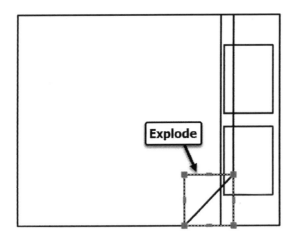

- Select the right vertical edge of the exploded rectangle; the Selection dialog appears.
- Select the right vertical edge of the exploded rectangle and press DELETE.
- Likewise, delete the bottom horizontal edge of the exploded rectangle.

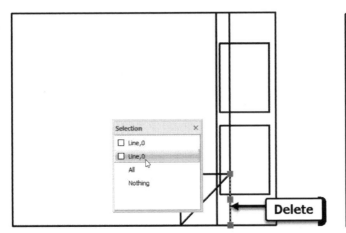

- On the menu bar, click **Modify** > **Trim Vectors**. Next, press ENTER.
- Trim the unwanted portions of the rectangles and offset lines, as shown.

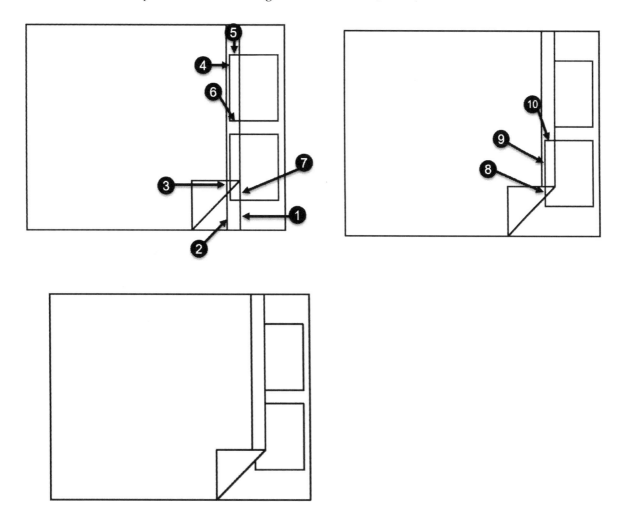

- On the menu bar, click **Draw** > **Block** > **Make**. Next, type **Dining Set** in the **Name** box on the **Block Definition** dialog.

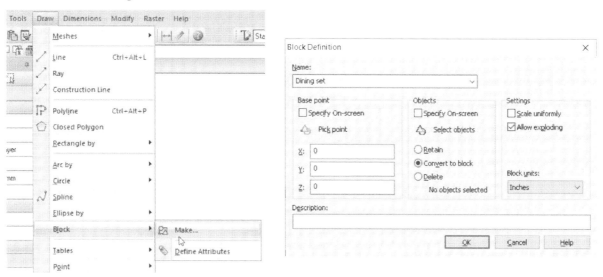

- Click the **Select objects** icon in the **Objects** section. Next, create a selection window across the dining set.

- Press ENTER and click the **Pick point** ⬦ icon in the **Base point** section.
- Select the lower-left corner of the rectangle, as shown.

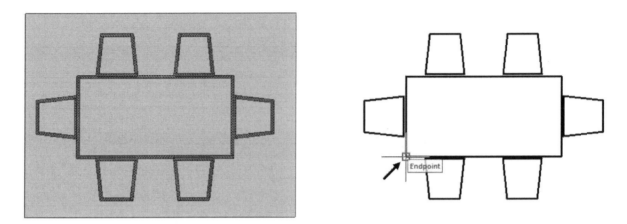

- Select the **Convert to Block** option and click **OK**.
- Select the Dining set block, and then click on the grip located at the bottom-left corner.
- Move the block and place it at the location shown below.

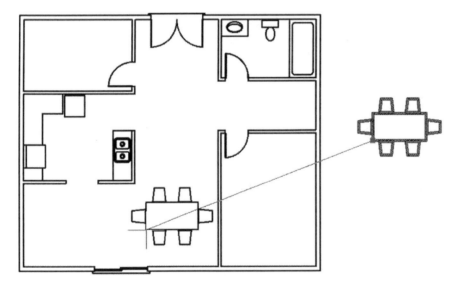

- On the menu bar, click **Draw > Block > Make**. Next, type **Bed** in the **Name** box on the **Block Definition** dialog.
- Click the **Select objects** ⬦ area icon in the **Objects** section. Next, create a selection window across the bed.
- Press ENTER and click the **Pick point** ⬦ icon in the **Base point** section.
- Select the lower-left corner of the rectangle, as shown.

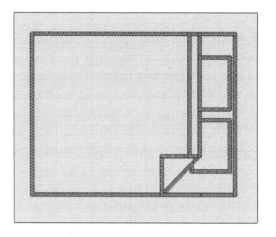
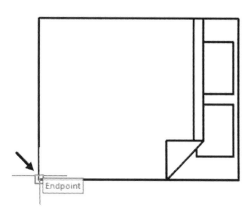

- Select the **Convert to Block** option and click **OK**.

- Activate the **Rectangle by Two Points** command and select the corner point of the bedroom, as shown.

- Right click and select the **Dimensions** option from the shortcut menu. Next, specify **86** and **27.5** as the length and width dimensions of the rectangle, respectively.

- Move the pointer downward and click create the rectangle.

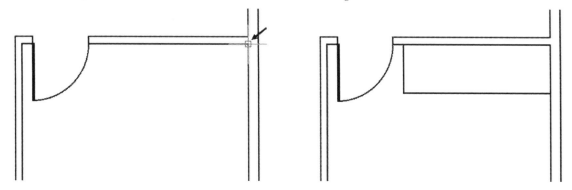

- Create another rectangle by selecting the corner points, as shown below.

- Offset the rectangle by a distance of **47.5** inwards. Next, delete the original rectangle.

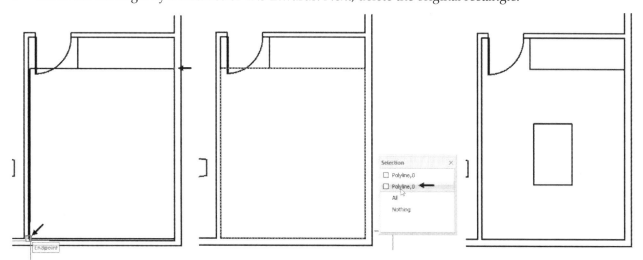

- Select the bed and click on the grip located at the bottom left corner.

- Move the pointer and select the bottom left corner of the offset rectangle to define the destination point.

- Press Esc and delete the offset rectangle.

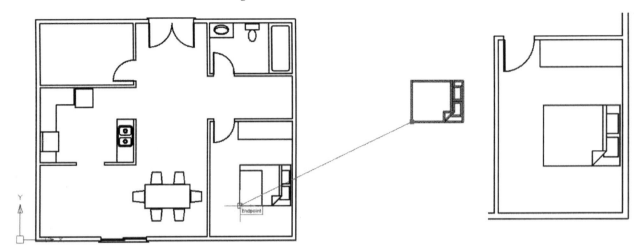

Adding Windows

- In the empty space, create the window using the **Line** command, as shown below.

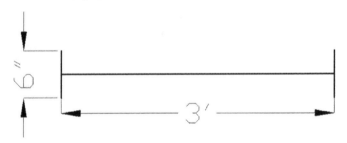

- On the menu bar, click **Draw > Block**.
- On the **Block Definition** dialog, type-in **Window** in the **Name** box.
- Click the **Select objects** ✍ area icon in the **Entities** section. Next, create a selection window across all the newly created elements.
- Press ENTER and click the **Pick point** ✍ icon in the **Base point** section.
- Select the lower-left corner of the window.

- Make sure that the **Convert to Block** option is selected under the **Entities** section.
- Click **OK** on the **Block Definition** dialog.
- On the menu bar, click **Draw > Construction Line**.
- Right click and select **Offset**. Next, type 95 and press ENTER.
- Select the right vertical line, as shown. Next, move the pointer toward the left and click.

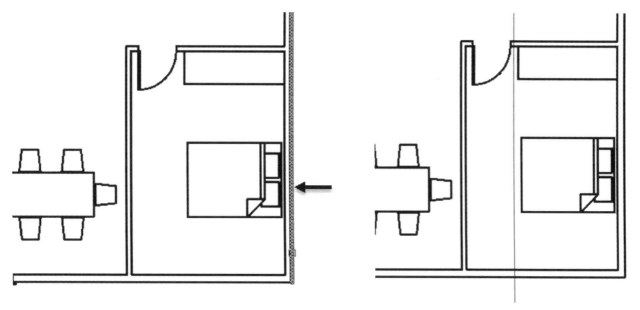

- Press ENTER twice. Next, right click and select **Offset** from the shortcut menu.

- Type 26 and press ENTER. Next, select the horizontal line of the kitchen wall, as shown.

- Move the pointer upward and click.

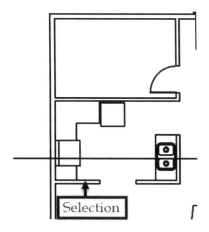

- Press ENTER twice. Next, right click and select **Offset** from the shortcut menu.

- Type 29 and press ENTER. Next, select the horizontal line, as shown.

- Move the pointer upward and click.

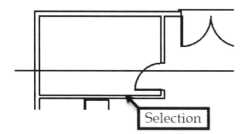

- Press ENTER twice. Next, right click and select **Offset** from the shortcut menu.

- Type 16 and press ENTER. Next, select the horizontal line, as shown.

- Move the pointer upward and click.

- Press ENTER twice. Next, right click and select **Offset** from the shortcut menu.

- Type 54 and press ENTER. Next, select the vertical line, as shown.
- Move the pointer toward the right and click.

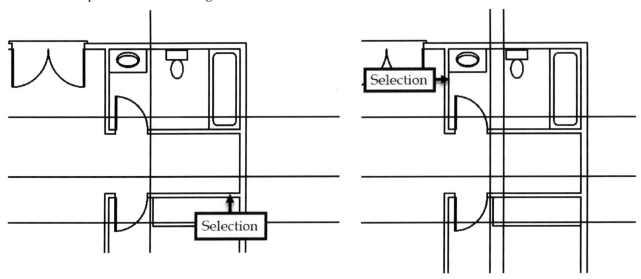

- On the menu bar, click **Insert > Block**. Next, select **Window** from the **Name** drop-down.
- Type 1.5 in the **X** box available in the **Scale** section. Next, click **OK**.

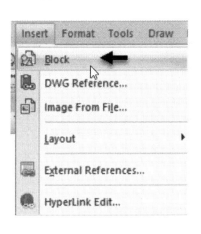

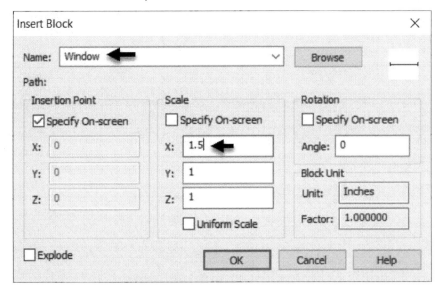

- Select the intersection point between the construction line and the horizontal line, as shown. The **Window** block will be placed at the specified location.

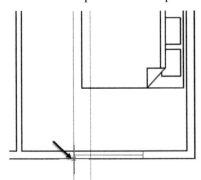

- Press ENTER and select **Window** from the **Name** drop-down.
- Type 0.72 in the **X** box available in the **Scale** section. Next, click **OK**.

- Select the intersection point between the infinite line and the horizontal line, as shown.

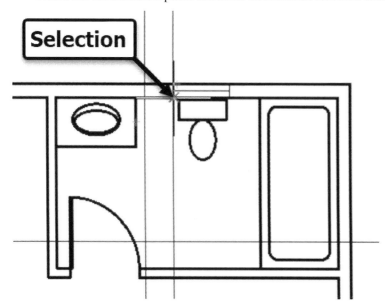

- On the menu bar, click **Insert > Block**. Next, select **Window** from the **Name** drop-down.

- Type-in the **90 Angle** box and click **OK**.

- Place the **Window** block on the kitchen wall, as shown below.

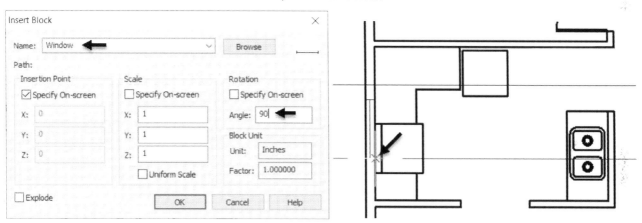

- Likewise, place the window blocks, as shown below.

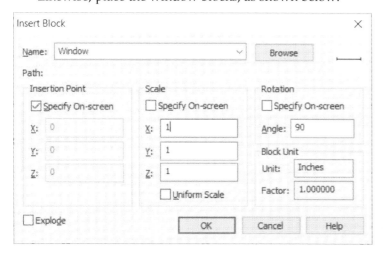

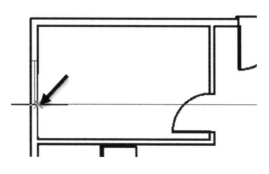

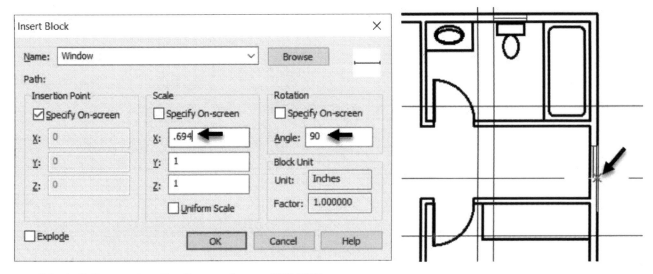

- Select all the construction lines and press DELETE.

Arranging Objects of the drawing in Layers

- On the menu bar, click **Format > Layers**. It displays the **Layers** dialog.
- On the **Layers** dialog, click the **Add** button.

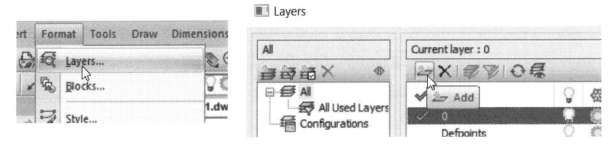

- Type **Wall** in the layer **Name** box and press Enter.
- Create another layer, and then type-in **Door** − press Enter.
- Likewise, create other layers, as shown below.

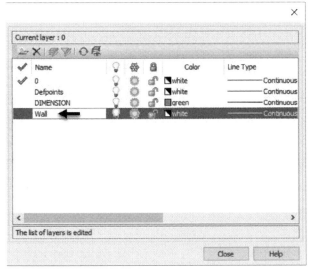
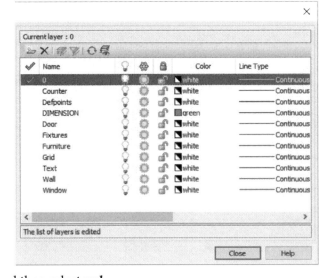

- Click the **Color** drop-down of the **Counter** layer, and then select **red**.

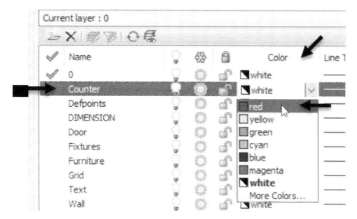

- Click the **Color** drop-down of the **Dimensions** layer, and then select the **More Colors** option.

- Select the **Index color 8** from the **Select Color** dialog. Next, click **OK**.

- Likewise, change the line colors of the remaining layers, as shown. Next, click the **Close** button.

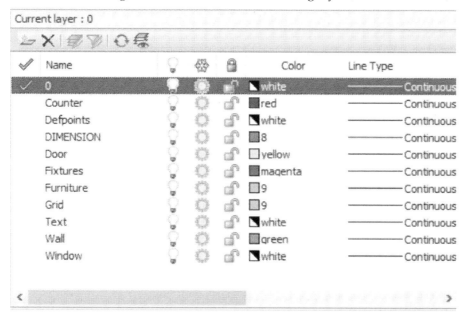

- On the menu bar, click **Format > Style**. Next, click the **Load Linetype** icon on the **Linetype Manager** dialog.

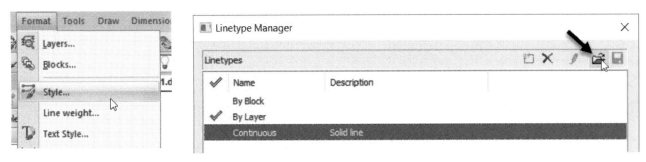

- Select the **ncad-in** file from the **Open Line Type Import** dialog. Click **Open**.

- Select the **DASHED** Linetype from the **Load Linetypes** dialog. Next, click **OK** twice.

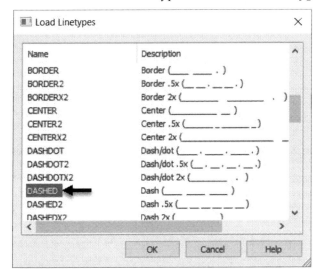

- On the menu bar, click **Format > Layers**. It displays the **Layers** dialog.

- Click the **Line Type** drop-down of the **Grid** layer, and then select **DASHED**.

- Click the **Line Weight** drop-down of the **Counter** layer and select 0.35 mm.

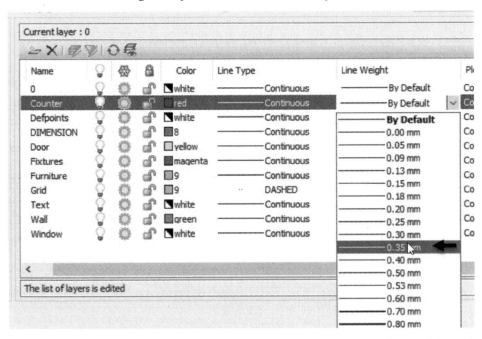

- Likewise, change the Line weights of the remaining layers, as shown. Next, close the **Layers** dialog.

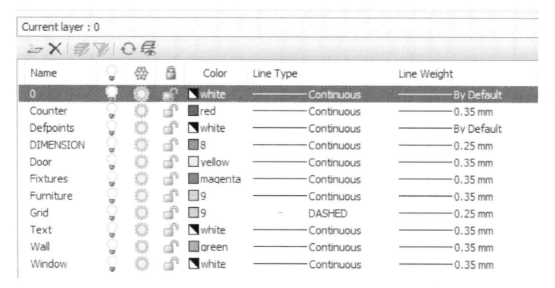

- Press and hold the SHIFT key and select the Dining set, cupboard, and bed.

- On the Properties toolbar, click **Layers > Furniture**. The selected objects will be transferred to the **Furniture** layer.

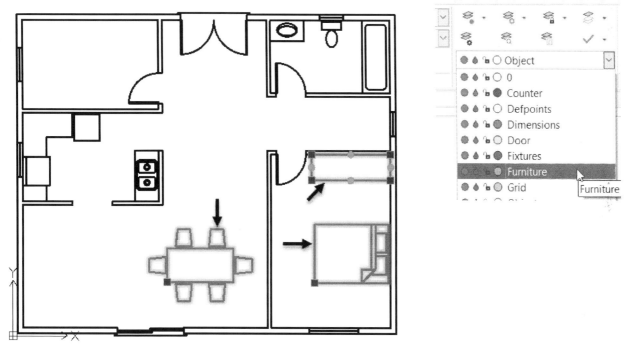

- Press Esc to deselect the selected objects.

- Press and hold the SHIFT key and select the kitchen and bathroom fixtures. Next, click **Layers > Fixtures** on the **Properties** toolbar.

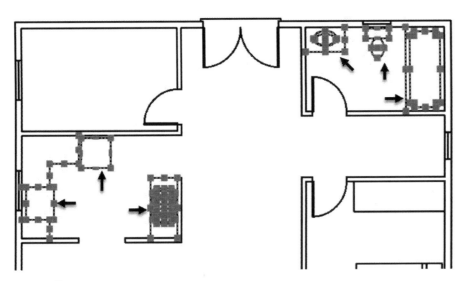

- Press Esc.
- Likewise, transfer the remaining objects onto their respective layers, as shown.

- Open the **Layers** dialog and click the bulb icons associated with Door, Window, Fixtures, Furniture, and Counter layers. It will hide the corresponding layers.

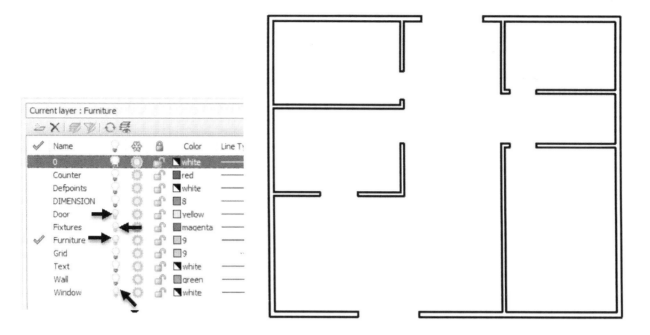

- Create a selection window and select all the walls.
- On the Properties toolbar, click **Layers > Wall**. All the walls will be transferred to the **Wall** layer.

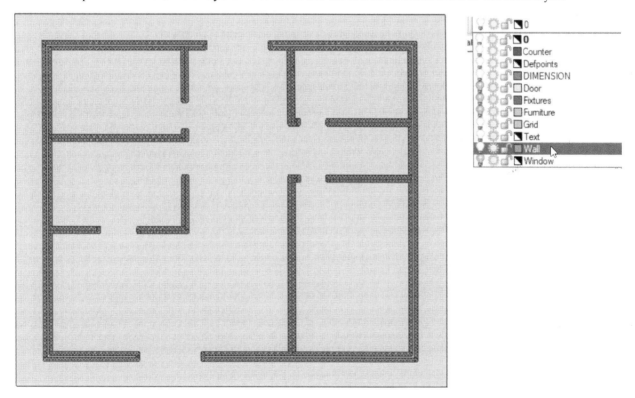

- Now, turn ON the hidden layers by clicking the bulb symbols on the Layers drop-down of the **Properties** toolbar.

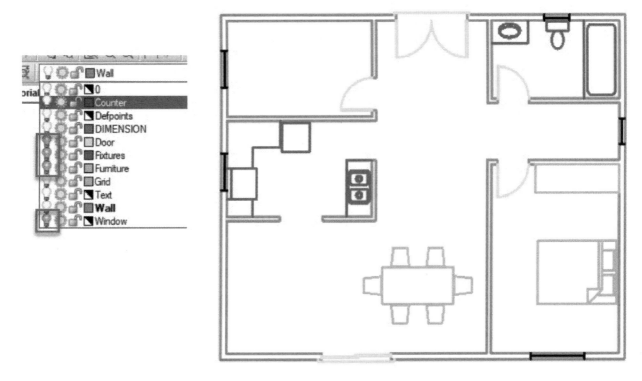

Creating Grid Lines

- On the Properties toolbar, click **Layers > Grid**. The **Grid** layer becomes active.

- Click **Draw > Construction Line** on the menu bar. Next, select the **Ver** option from the command line.

- Select the endpoint of the window left outer wall, as shown.

- Zoom to the top portion of the drawing and the selected midpoint of the inner wall's horizontal edge.

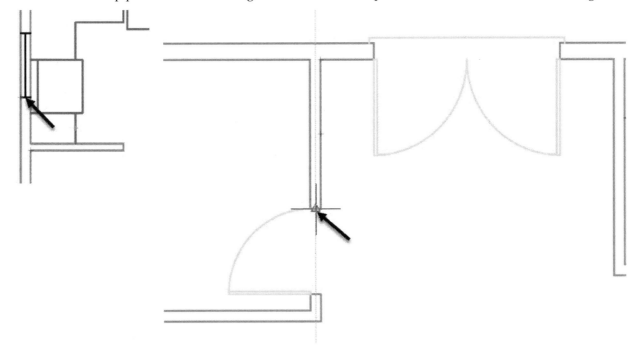

- Select the endpoint of the window of the right outer wall.

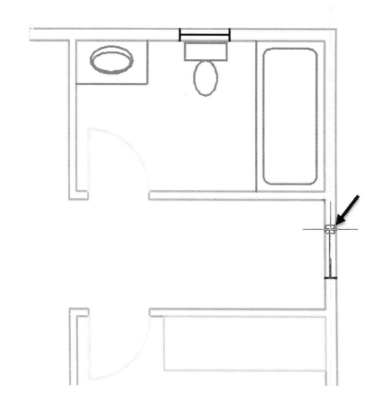

- Press ENTER twice and select the **Offset** option from the command line.

- Type 2 in the command line and press ENTER.

- Select the vertical edge of the inner wall, as shown. Next, move the pointer toward the right and click.

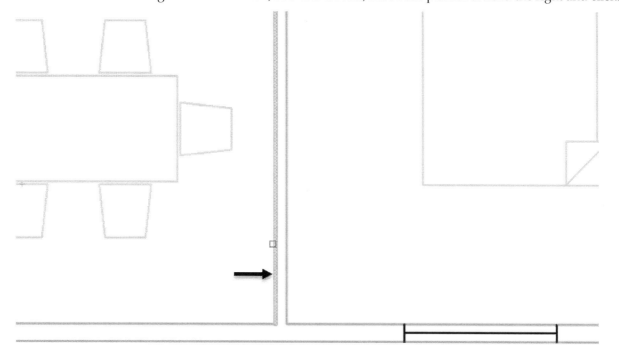

- Select the horizontal edge of the inner wall, as shown. Next, move the pointer downward and click.

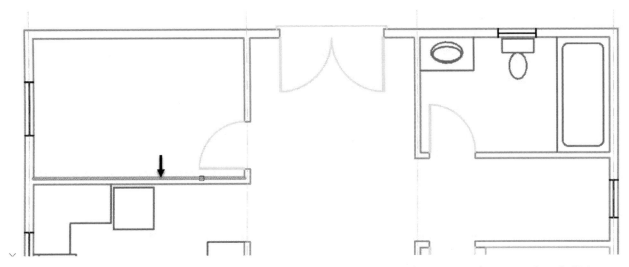

- Select the horizontal edge of the inner wall, as shown. Next, move the pointer downward and click.
- Select the horizontal edge of the inner wall, as shown. Next, move the pointer downward and click.

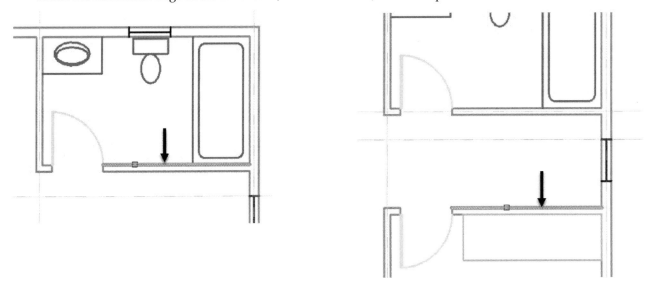

- Select the horizontal edge of the inner wall, as shown. Next, move the pointer downward and click.

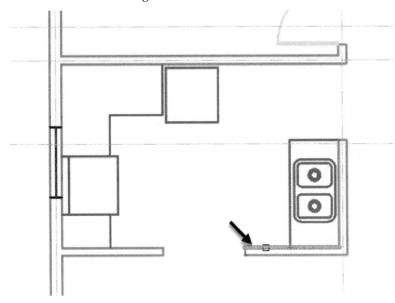

- Press ENTER twice and select the **Hor** option from the command line.

- Select the endpoints of the windows of the outer walls, as shown. Next, press ENTER twice.

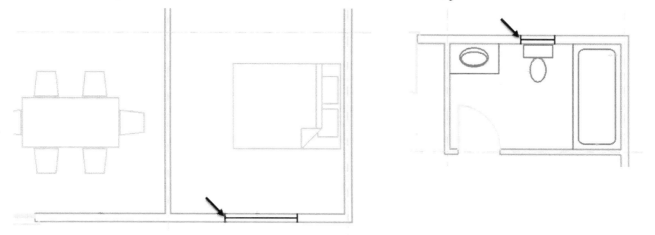

- Select the **Offset** option from the command line. Next, type 36 and press ENTER.
- Select the left vertical dotted line. Next, move the pointer toward the left and click.
- Select the top horizontal dotted line. Next, move the pointer upward and click.

- Select the bottom horizontal dotted line. Next, move the pointer downward and click.
- Select the right vertical dotted line. Next, move the pointer toward the right and click.

- On the menu bar, click **Modify > Trim Vectors**. Next, press ENTER to select all the elements as the cutting edges.
- Press and hold the left mouse button and drag the pointer from right to left across the top portions of the vertical dotted lines.
- Press and hold the left mouse button and drag the pointer from right to left across the right portions of the horizontal dotted lines.

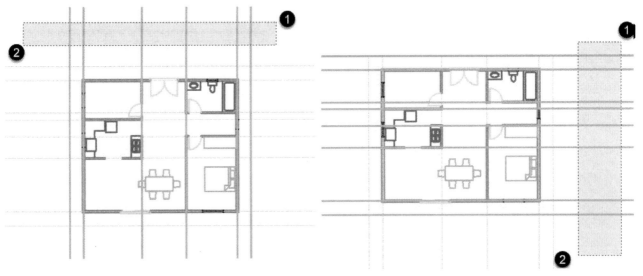

- Press and hold the left mouse button and drag the pointer from right to left across the vertical dotted lines' bottom portions.
- Press and hold the left mouse button and drag the pointer from right to left across the left portions of the horizontal dotted lines.

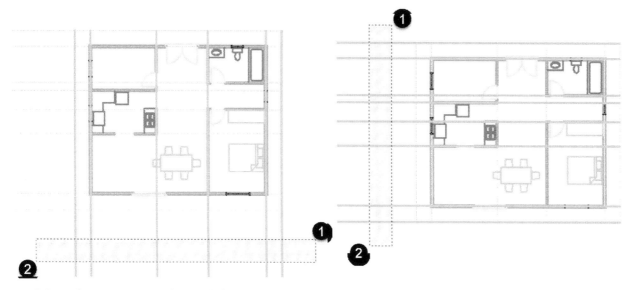

- Move the point upward and click to draw a vertical line of arbitrary length.

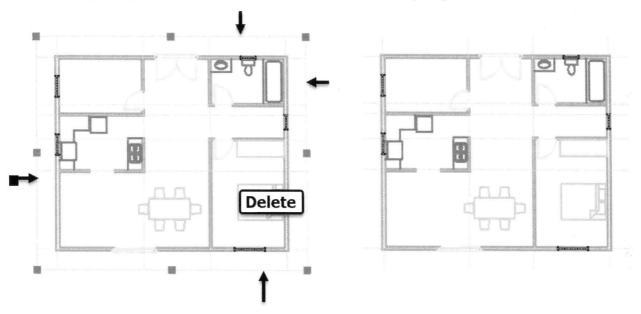

- Create a new layer called **Grid Bubble**. Next, right-click on the **Grid Bubble** layer and select **Set Current**.

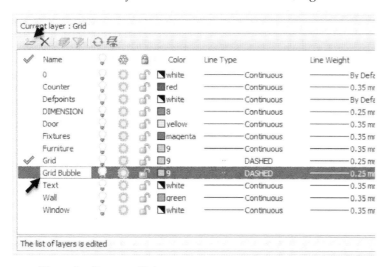

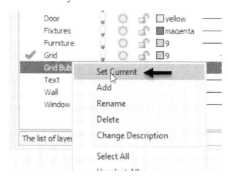

- Close the **Layers** dialog.

- Create a circle of 12 diameter.

- On the menu bar, click **Draw > Block > Define Attributes**.

- On the **Attribute Definition** dialog, type-in GRIDBUBBLE in the **Tag** box and select **Justification > Middle center**.

- Type-in **6** in the **Text Height** box and click **OK**.

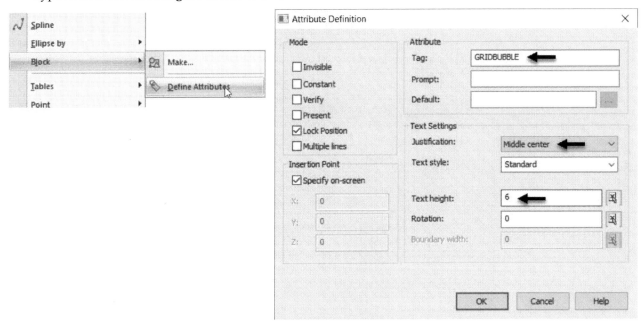

- Select the center point of the circle. The attribute text will be placed at its center.

- On the menu bar, click **Draw > Block > Make**.

- Type-in Grid bubble in the **Name** box and click the **Select objects** button under the **Objects** section.

- Draw a crossing window to select the circle and attribute. Press Enter to accept the selection.

- Click the **Pick point** icon under the **Base point** section.

- Press and hold the SHIFT key and right-click. Next, select the **Quadrant** option.

- Select the lower quadrant point of the circle to define the base point of the block.

- Select the **Delete** option from the **Objects** section and click **OK**.
- On the menu bar, click **Insert > Block**. Next, select the **Grid Bubble** block from the **Name** drop-down.
- Type **0** in the **Angle** box and click **OK**.
- Select the top endpoint of the first vertical grid line.
- Type-in **A** in the command line and press ENTER.

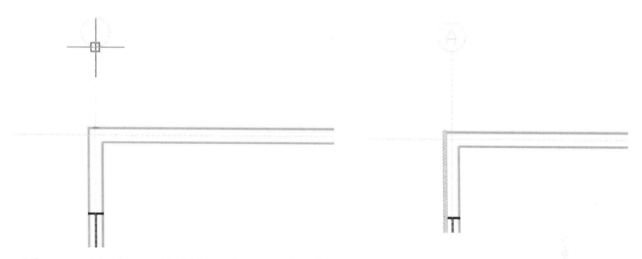

- Likewise, add other grid bubbles to the vertical grid lines.

- Create another block with the name Vertical Grid bubble. Make sure that you select the right quadrant point of the circle as the base point.

- Insert the vertical grid bubbles, as shown below.

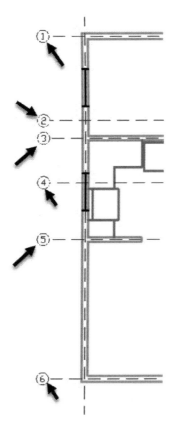

Adding Dimensions

- On the **Properties** toolbar, click **Layers > DIMENSION** to make it current.

- Click **Format > Dimension Styles** on the menu bar.

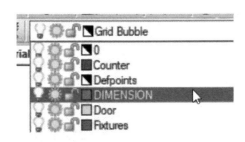
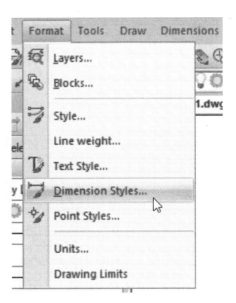

- On the **Dimension Style Manager** dialog, select the **Standard** dimension style and click the **New** button.

- Type-in **Floor Plan** in the **New Style Name** box and click **OK**.

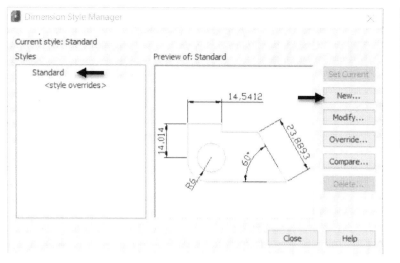

- Click the **Primary Units** tab and select **Unit format > Architectural**.

- Set **Precision** to **0′-01/16″**.

- Set **Fraction format** to **Horizontal**.

- Under the **Zero Suppression** section, uncheck the **0 inches** option.

- Click the **Symbols and arrows** tab.

- Under the **Arrowheads** section, select **First > Architectural tick**. The second arrowhead is automatically changed to **Architectural tick**.

- Select **Leader > Closed Filled** and enter 1/4′ in the **Arrow Size** box.

- Click the **Lines** tab and set **Extend beyond dim lines** and **Offset from origin** to 3″.

- Click the **Text** tab and **Text height** to 6″.

- In the **Text placement** section, set the following settings.
  Vertical-Centered
  Horizontal-Centered

- In the **Text alignment** section, select the **Aligned with dimension line** option.

- Click the **Fit** tab, and select the **Either text or arrows (best fit)** option from the **Fit Options** section.

- In the **Text placement** section, select the **Over dimension line without Leader** option.

- Click **OK** and click **Set Current** on the **Dimension Style Manager**. Click **Close**.

- Click the **Dimension** icon on the **Utilities** toolbar.

- Select the points on the vertical grid lines, as shown below.

- Move the pointer and click to locate the dimension.

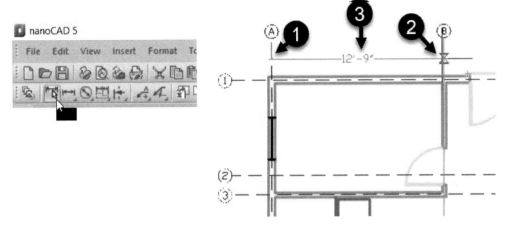

- On the menu bar, click **Dimensions > Dimension Chain**. Next, select the existing dimension; you will notice that a dimension is attached to the pointer.

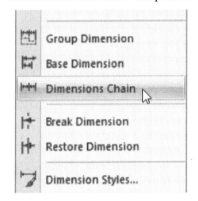

- Move the pointer and click on the next grid line.

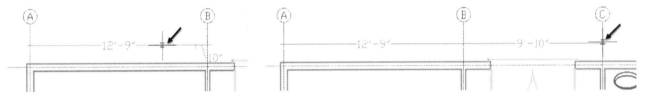

- Likewise, move the pointer and click on the next grid line.

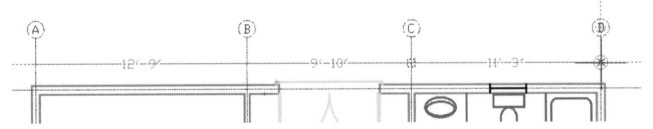

- On the menu bar, click **Dimensions > Base Dimension**. Select the last dimension of the dimension chain.
- Move the pointer and select the left vertical grid line. Next, press ESC.

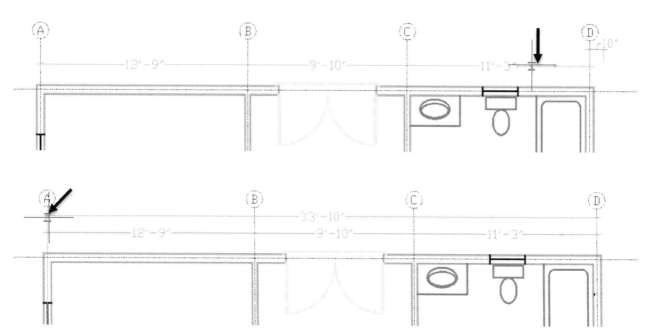

- Likewise, add vertical dimensions to the grid lines.

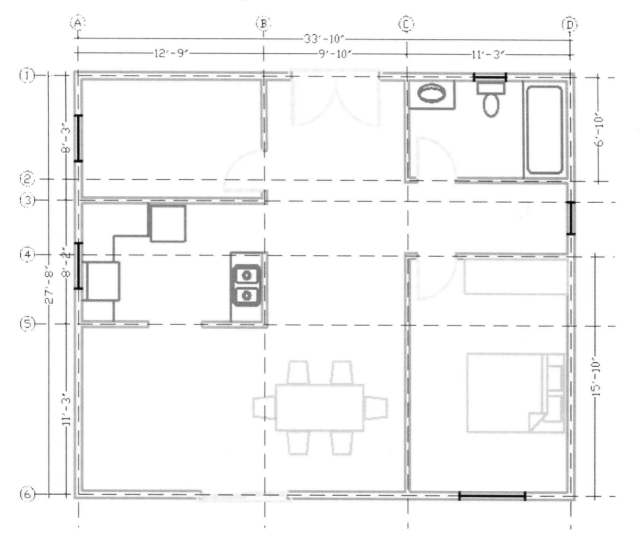

- Save and close the drawing.

Tutorial 2: Creating the Stairs

In this tutorial, you will draw stairs.

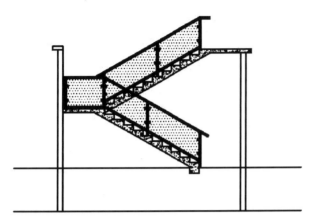

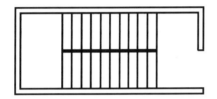

Staircase Nomenclature

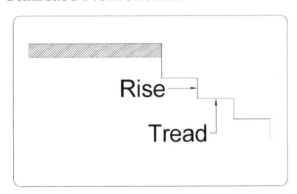

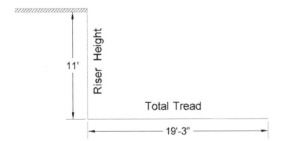

Creating the Stairs

- Click **File > New Document** on the menu bar.
- On the menu bar, click the **Format > Units**. The **Drawing Units** dialog appears.

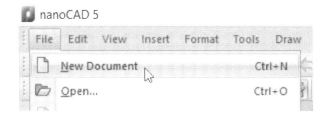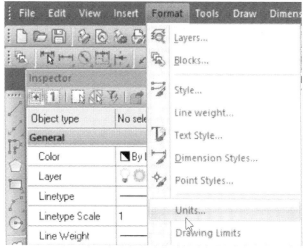

- On the **Drawing Units** dialog, select **Type > Architectural** from the **Length** section.

- Select **Precision > 0-01/16**. Next, set the **Units to scale inserted content** to **Inches**, and click **OK**.

- Type LIMITS in the command line and press Enter.

- Press Enter to accept 0, 0 as the lower limit.

- Type 50', 40' in the command line, and press Enter. The program sets the upper limit of the drawing.

- On the menu bar, click the **View > Zoom > Zoom Extents**.

- Deactivate the **Grid** icon on the status bar.

- Activate the **ORTHO** icon on the Status bar.
- Click **Draw > Polyline** on the menu bar.
- Click to define the start point of the line. Next, move the pointer toward the left.
- Type 17'8" and press ENTER.

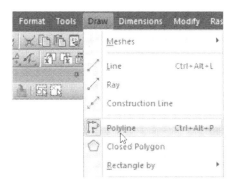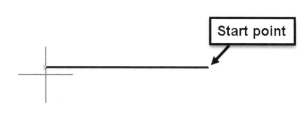

- Move the pointer upward. Next, type 7' and press ENTER.
- Move the pointer toward the right. Next, type 17'2" and press ENTER.

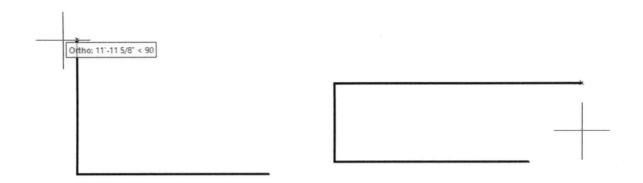

- Move the pointer downward. Next, type 3'6" and press ENTER.
- Press Esc.

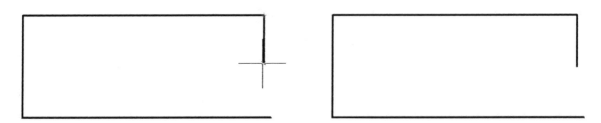

- On the menu bar, click the **Modify > Offset** tool. Next, type 6" and press ENTER.
- Select the polyline. Next, move the pointer outward and click.
- Click the **Line by Points** tool on the **Draw** toolbar and close the drawing's open ends, as shown.

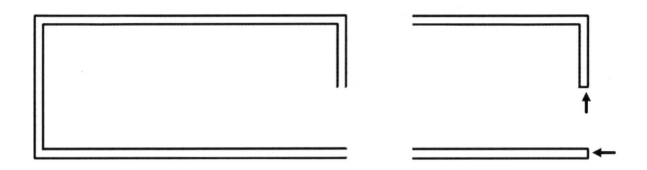

- Create a selection window across all the elements of the drawing.

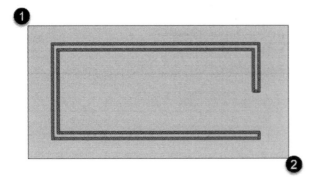

- Click the **Explode** icon on the **Modify** toolbar. The polylines are exploded into lines.

- Click **Modify > Offset** 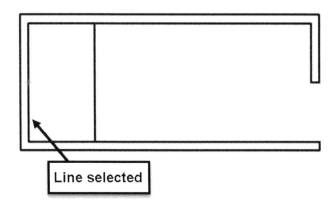 on the menu bar. Next, type 4′ and press ENTER.
- Select the left vertical inner edge. Next, move the pointer toward the right and click.

Line selected

- Press ENTER.
- On the menu bar, click **Modify > Array**; the **Array** dialog appears on the screen.

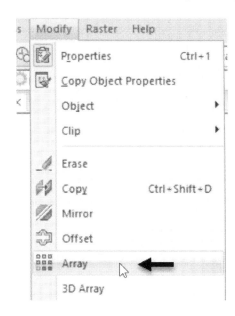

- Select the **Rectangular Array** option. Next, type **1** in the **Rows** box and type **11** in the **Columns** box.
- Type **11** in the **Column offset** box under the **Offset distance and direction** section on the dialog.
- Click the **Select Objects** selection arrow located at the top right corner of the dialog.
- Select the offset line and press Enter. Next, click **OK** on the **Array** dialog.

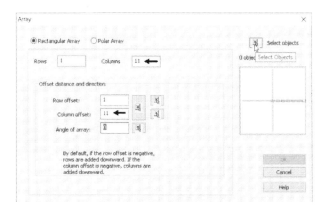

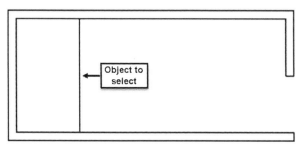

Object to select

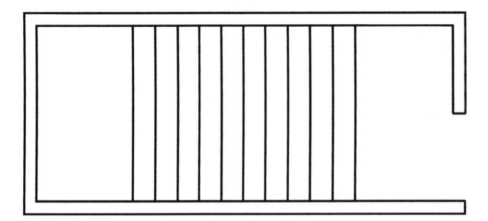

- Activate the **Offset** command and type **3'5"** in the command line. Press Enter.
- Select the inner horizontal line, as shown. Next, move the pointer upward and click to create the offset line and press Esc.

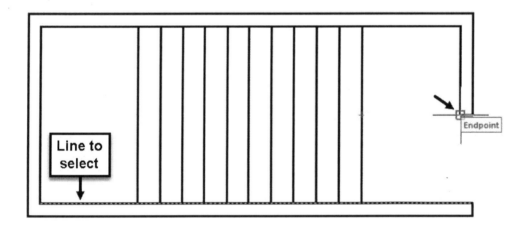

- Again, activate the **Offset** command and type **1** in the command line. Press Enter.
- Select the newly created offset line and then click on the top portion of the drawing.

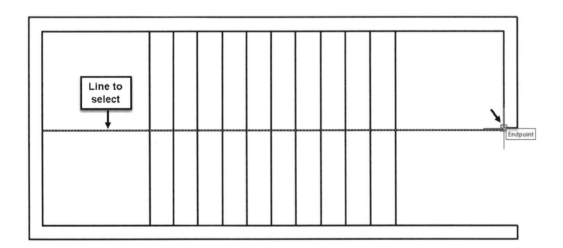

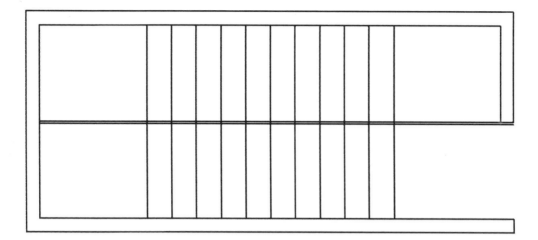

- On the menu bar, click **Modify** panel > **Trim Vectors**. Next, press Enter to select all the objects.
- Create a crossing window from right to left across the horizontal lines' unwanted portions, as shown.
- Likewise, trim the unwanted portions of the horizontal lines, as shown.

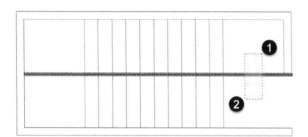
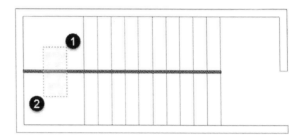

- Zoom-in to the center portion of the stairs. Click on the portions of the vertical lines, as shown.

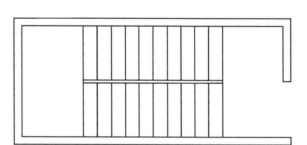

Creating the Section elevation of the Staircase

- Create a horizontal line above the staircase, as shown.
- Click the **Modify > Offset** on the menu bar tab. Next, type **4'** and press ENTER.
- Select the newly created horizontal line. Move the pointer upward and click to create the offset line.

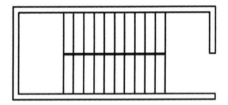 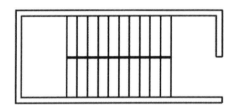

- On the menu bar, click **Draw > Construction Line**. Next, select the **Ver** option from the command line.
- Select the endpoints of the left vertical line, as shown.
- Likewise, select the endpoints of the lines, as shown. Next, press ESC.

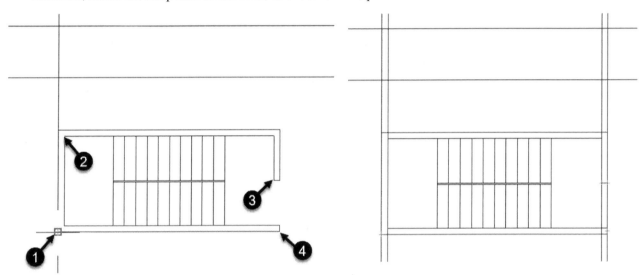

- Click the **Modify** tab > **Offset** on the menu bar. Next, type 10'8" and press ENTER.
- Select the offset horizontal line. Next, move the pointer upward and click.

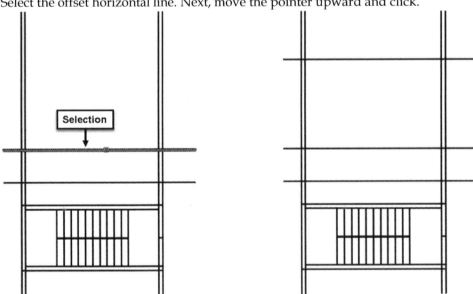

- Press ENTER twice to deactivate the **Offset** tool and then activate it again. Next, type 4" and press ENTER.

- Select the newly created offset line. Next, move the pointer upward and click.

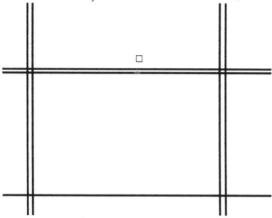

- Press **Esc** to deactivate the **Offset** tool.
- On the menu bar, click **Modify > Trim Vectors**. Press ENTER.
- Press and hold the left mouse button and drag the selection box from right to left across the construction lines' portions, as shown.

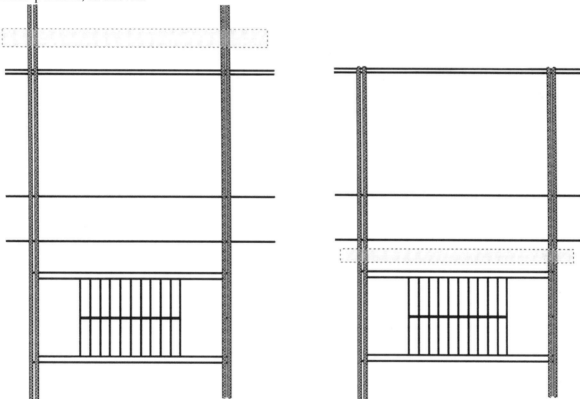

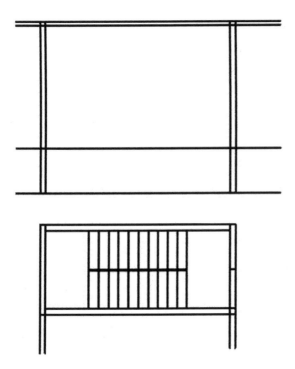

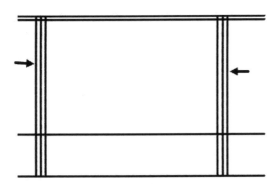

- Click **Modify >Offset** on the menu bar. Next, type **6″** and press ENTER.
- Offset the outer vertical lines on both sides.

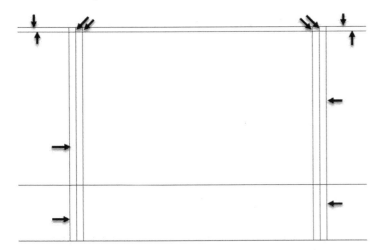

- On the menu bar, click **Modify > Trim Vectors**. Next, press ENTER.
- Trim the portions of the vertical and horizontal lines, as shown.

- On the menu bar, click **Modify > Extend Vectors**.
- Select the lower horizontal edge of the roof, as shown. Next, press ENTER.

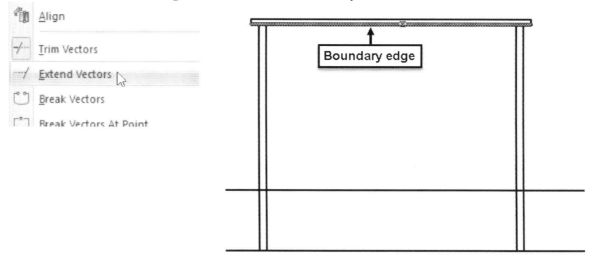

- Press and hold the left mouse button.
- Create a selection window across the staircase lines from right to left; the lines are extended up to the boundary edge.

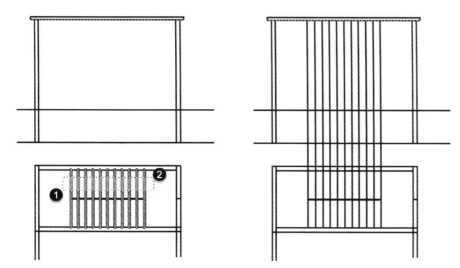

- On the menu bar, click **Modify > Trim Vector**.
- Press and hold the SHIFT key and select the horizontal lines, as shown. Next, press ENTER.
- Create a selection window across the vertical lines, as shown.

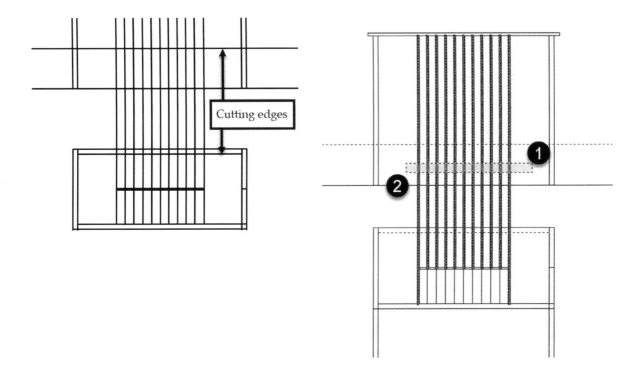

- On the menu bar, click **Draw > Polyline**. Next, select the first point of the polyline.
- Move the pointer upward. Next, type 6" and press ENTER.
- Move the pointer toward the left. Next, type 11" and press ENTER.
- Press Esc.

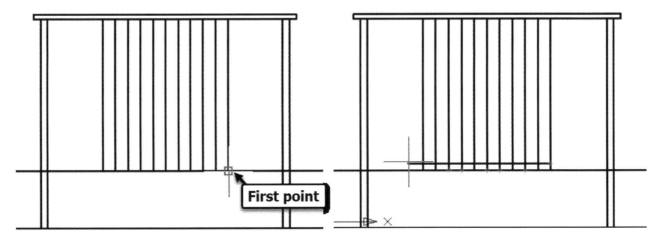

- Select the polyline and click the **Move Copy** icon on the **Modify** toolbar.
- Select the first point of the polyline as the base point.
- Move the pointer upward and select the endpoint of the polyline. The polyline is copied.

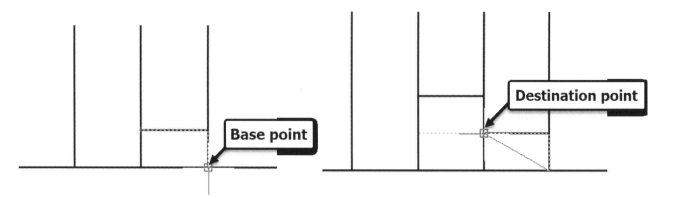

- Likewise, create copies of the polylines, as shown. Next, press ESC.

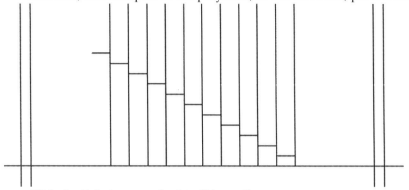

- Click the **Join** icon on the **Modify** toolbar.
- Press and hold the Shift key and select all the polylines, and press ENTER. All the polylines are joined.

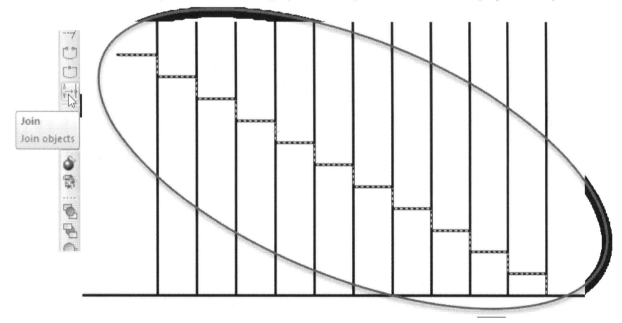

- On the menu bar, click **Modify > Extend Vectors**. Next, press ENTER.
- Click on the end portion of the polyline to extend it up to the left vertical line. Press Esc.

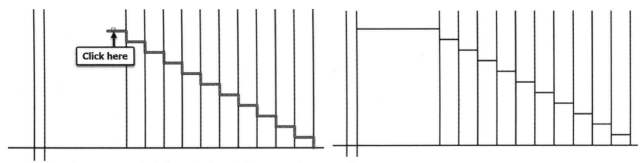

- Select the stairs and click **Modify > Mirror** on the menu bar.
- Specify the start point of the mirror line, as shown.
- Move the pointer toward the left and specify the endpoint of the mirror line, as shown. Next, select **No**.

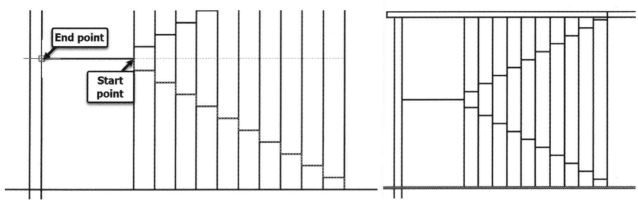

- Select the mirrored polyline. Next, click on the endpoint of the polyline.
- Move the pointer toward the right and select the vertex point, as shown. The polyline is shortened.

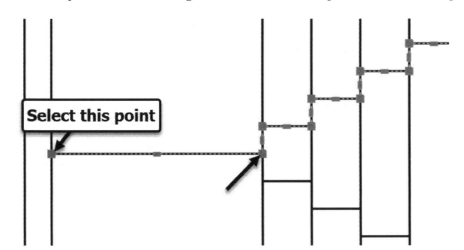

- Press Esc to deselect the mirrored polyline.
- Drag a selection window across the vertical lines from right to left, as shown.

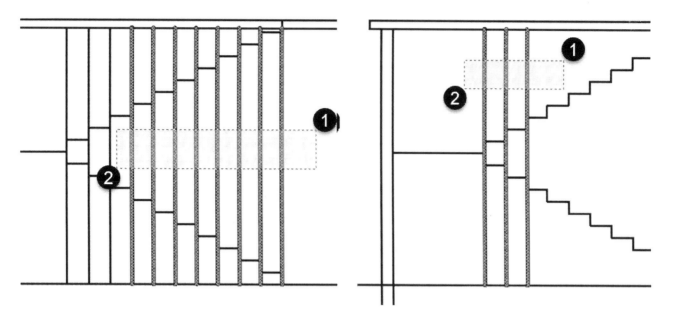

- Press Delete on your keyboard.
- On the menu bar, click **Draw** >**Line**. Next, select the corner points, as shown.
- Offset the newly created line by 4".

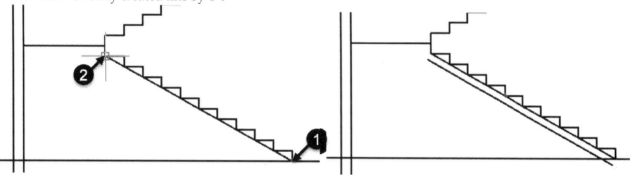

- On the menu bar, click **Draw** > **Line**. Next, select the two points, as shown.
- Press ESC and click on the newly created line.

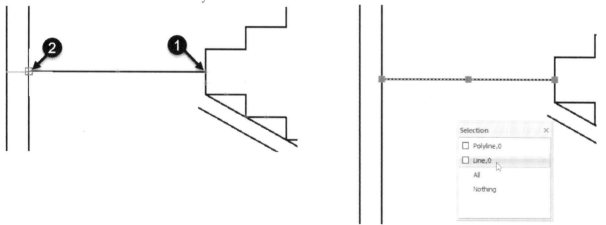

- Click on the midpoint of the selected line. Next, move the pointer downward and type 4. Next, press ENTER.

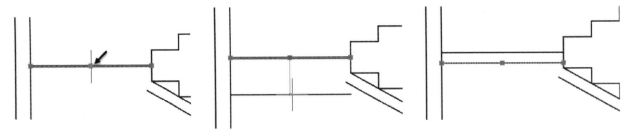

- Click the **Fillet** icon on the **Modify** toolbar. Type **0** in the **Radius** box and click **OK**.
- Select the horizontal and inclined lines, as shown.

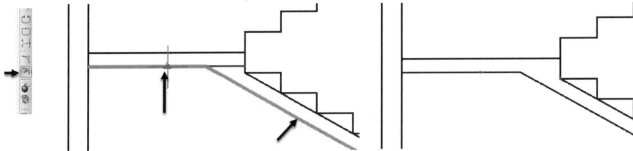

- Delete the inclined line, as shown.

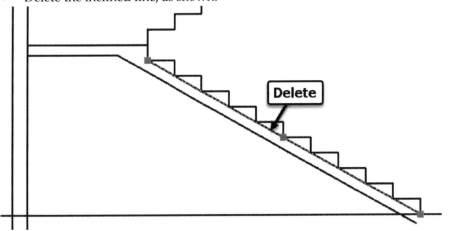

- On the menu bar, click **Draw > Line**. Next, select the corner point of the stair, as shown.
- Move the pointer downward. Next, type 1' and press ENTER.
- Move the pointer toward the right. Next, type 11" and press ENTER.
- Move the pointer upward. Next, type 6" and press ENTER.

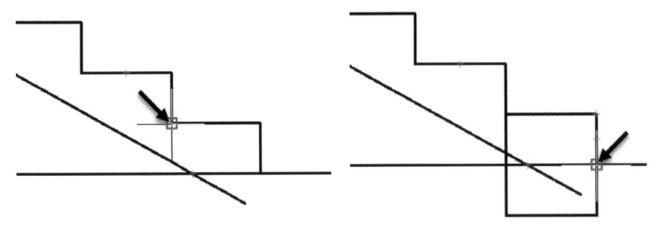

- On the menu bar, click **Modify > Trim Vectors**. Next, press ENTER.
- Select the portions of the lines, as shown.

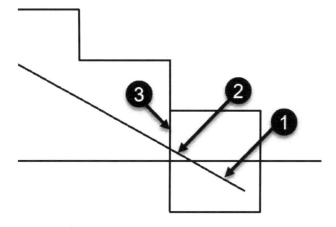

- On the menu bar, click **Draw** > **Line**. Select the corner points, as shown.
- Offset the newly created line by 4".

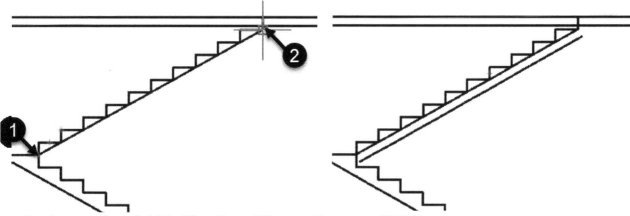

- On the menu bar, click **Modify** > **Extend Vectors**. Next, press ENTER.
- Select the inclined line, as shown.
- Extend the inclined line up to the horizontal line, as shown.

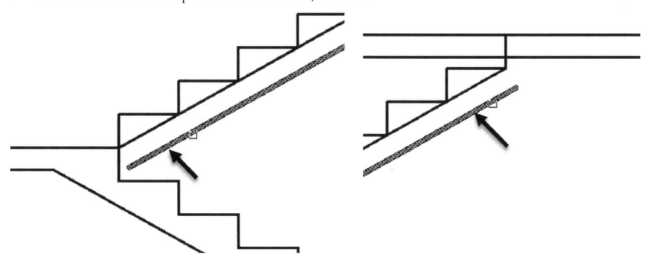

- Extend the vertical line, as shown. Next, press Esc.

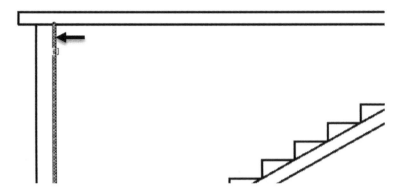

- Select the inclined line, as shown. Next, press Delete.

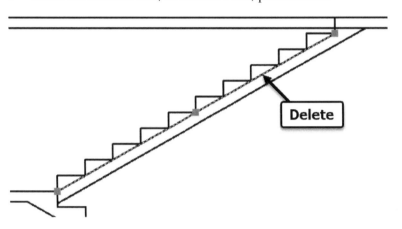

- On the menu bar, click **Modify > Trim Vectors**. Next, press ENTER.
- Click and drag the pointer across the entities, as shown.

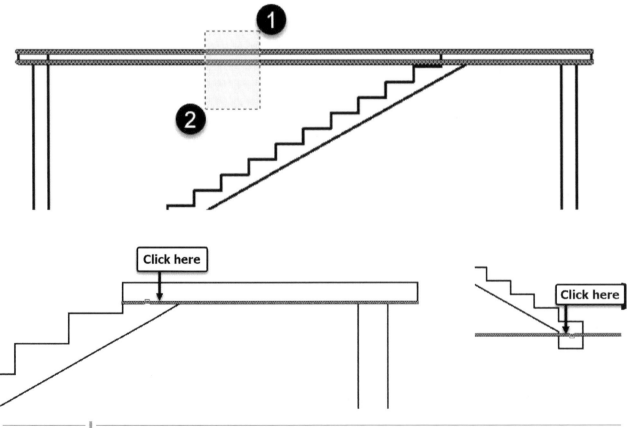

- On the menu bar, click **Draw > Hatch**.
- On the **Hatch** dialog, click the **Patterns** ⬚icon next to the **Pattern** drop-down,
- Click the **Other Predefined** tab on the **Hatch Pattern** dialog, and then select the **AR-CONC** pattern.

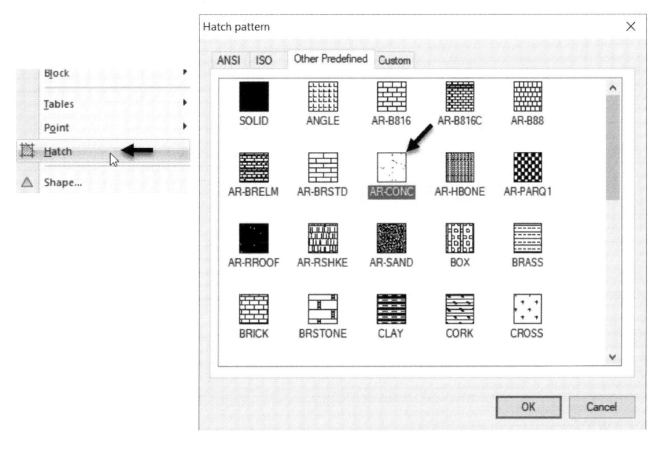

- Click **OK** on the **Hatch Pattern** dialog.
- Click the **Add: Pick points** icon under the **Boundary** section. Next, pick points in the areas, as shown.

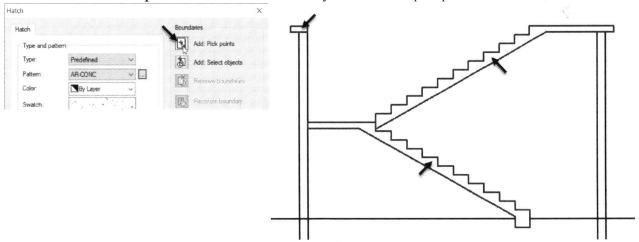

- Press ENTER.
- Type **0.05** in the **Scale** box under the **Angle and Scale** section and click **OK** on the **Hatch** dialog.

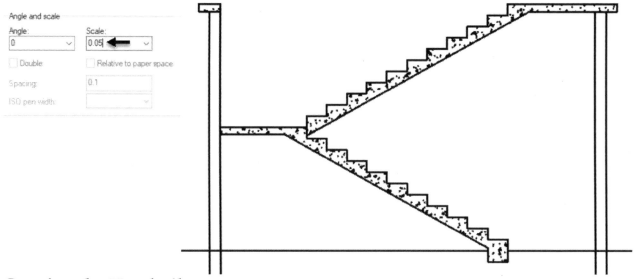

Creating the Handrail

- On the menu bar, click **Draw > Line**.
- Create two vertical lines of 3' length each at the locations, as shown.
- Activate the **Line** tool and connect the endpoints of the two vertical lines, as shown.

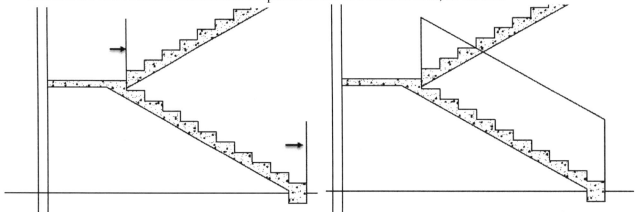

- On the menu bar, click **Modify > Lengthen objects**.
- Right-click and select **DElta**. Next, type 12" and press ENTER.

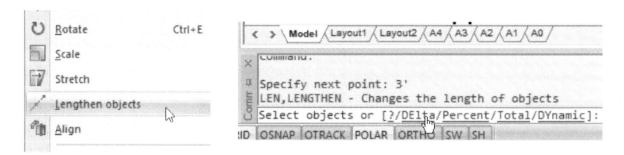

- Click near the endpoint of the inclined line. The inclined line is lengthened.

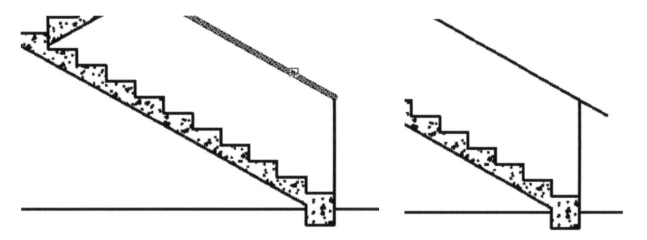

- Create a horizontal line, as shown.
- Click the **Offset** icon on the **Modify** toolbar. Next, offset the newly created lines by 2″ distance, as shown.

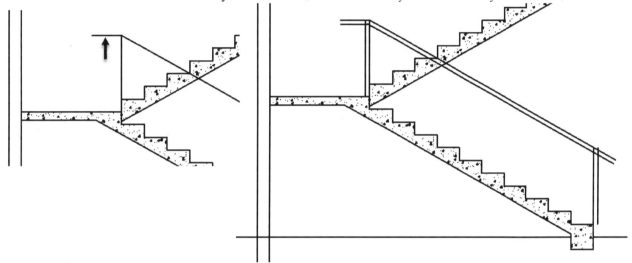

- On the menu bar, click **Modify** > **Extend Vectors**. Next, press ENTER.
- Extend the two vertical lines up to the bottom horizontal edge, as shown.

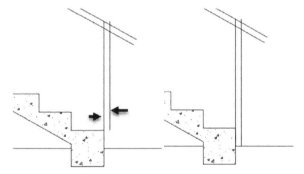

- Activate the **Line** tool. Next, zoom to the fifth step from the top.
- Select the midpoint of the horizontal line, as shown. Next, move the pointer upward and click.

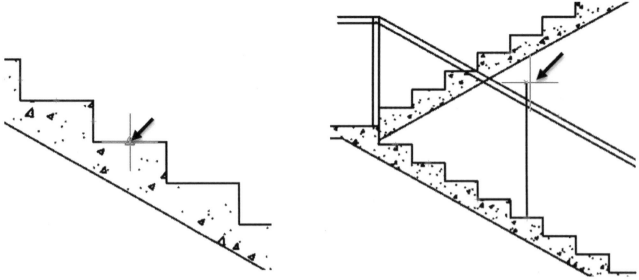

- Click the **Offset** icon on the **Modify** toolbar. Offset the newly created line by 1" on both sides, as shown.
- Delete the middle line.

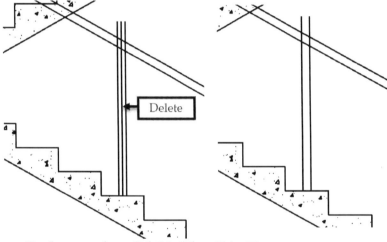

- On the menu bar, click **Modify > Trim Vectors**.
- Press and hold the SHIFT key and select the lower inclined and horizontal lines of the handrail. Next, press ENTER.
- Trim the portions of the vertical lines, as shown.

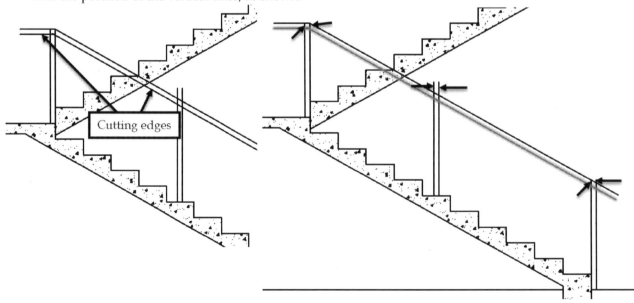

- Click the **Fillet** icon on the **Modify** toolbar. Type **0** in the **Radius** box and click **OK**.
- Select the horizontal and inclined lines, as shown.

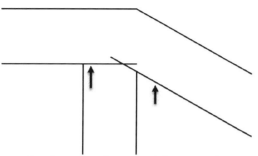

- On the menu bar, **Modify > Break Vectors At Point**.
- Select the vertical line, as shown.
- Select the midpoint of the vertical line, as shown. The vertical line is broken at the midpoint.

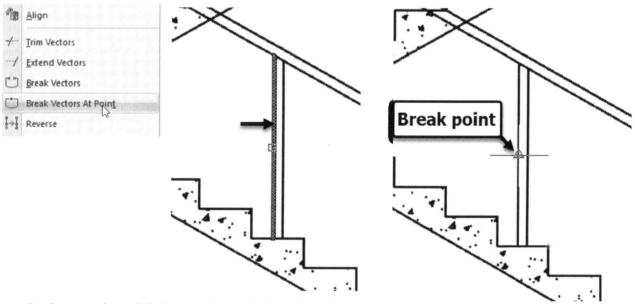

- On the menu bar, click **Draw > Rectangle by > Two Points**.
- Select the midpoint of the lower portion of the broken line, as shown.
- Right click and select the **Dimensions** option from the shortcut menu. Next, type 2 and press ENTER.
- Type 2 and press ENTER. Next, move the pointer upward and click.

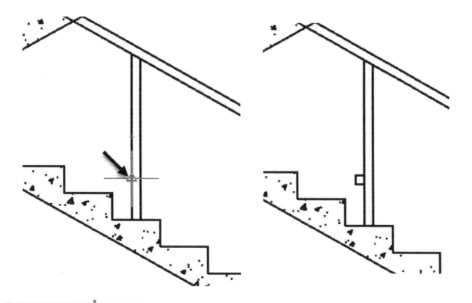

- Select the rectangle and click the **Move Copy** icon on the **Modify** toolbar.
- Select the top right corner point of the rectangle. Next, move the pointer upward.
- Select the midpoint of the upper portion of the broken line, as shown. Press ESC.

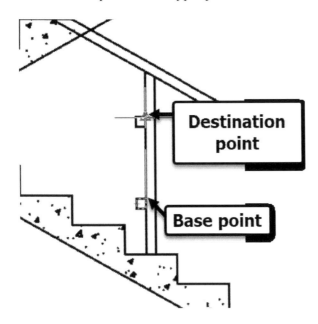

- Press and hold the SHIFT key, select the two rectangles and click the **Move Copy** icon on the **Modify** toolbar.
- Select the top right corner point of anyone of the rectangles.
- Move the pointer toward the right. Next, type 4" and press ENTER.
- Press ESC.

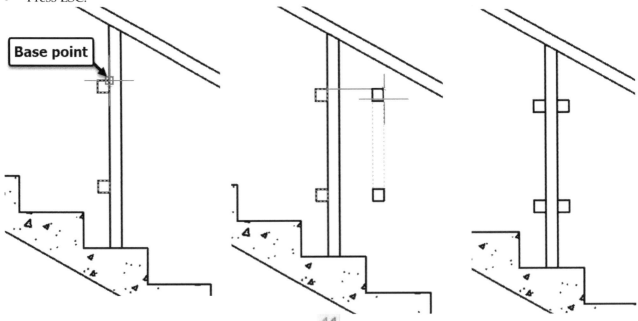

- Select the four rectangles and click the **Move Copy** icon on the **Modify** toolbar.
- Select the midpoint of the right vertical line.

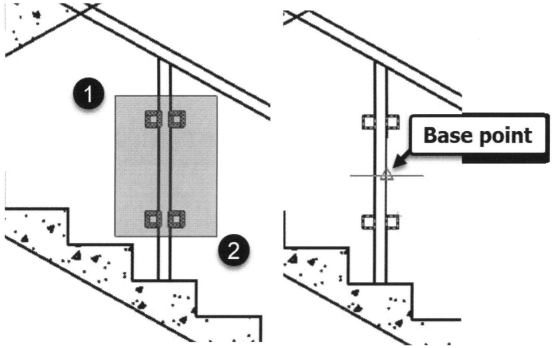

- Move the pointer toward the right and select the midpoint of the vertical line, as shown.
- Move the pointer toward the left and select the midpoint of the vertical line, as shown. Press Esc.

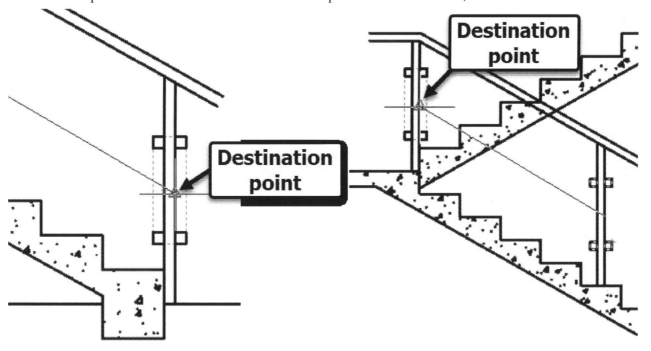

- Delete the two rectangles, as shown.

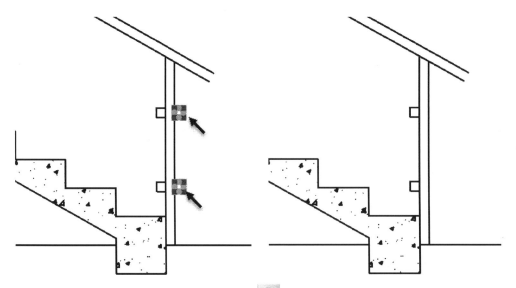

- Select the vertical line and click the **Offset** icon on the **Modify** toolbar.
- Type 3'8" and press ENTER. Next, move the pointer toward the left and click.
- Press ENTER twice.
- Type 2" and press ENTER. Next, select the newly offset line.
- Move the pointer toward the right and click.

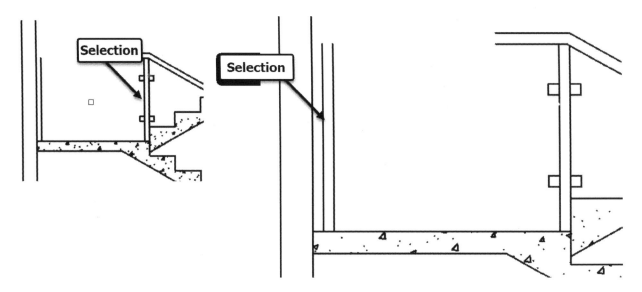

- Click the **Fillet** icon on the **Modify** toolbar. Next, type 0 in the **Radius** box and click **OK**.
- Select the left vertical and top horizontal line, as shown.

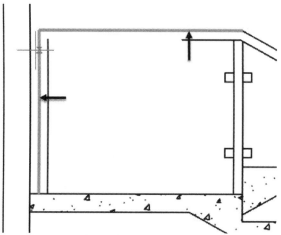

- On the menu bar, click **Modify > Extend Vectors**.
- Extend the horizontal line up to the vertical line. Press Esc.

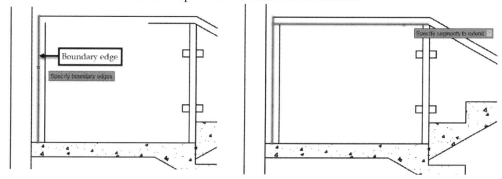

- Press and hold the SHIFT key and select the two rectangles.
- Click the **Move Copy** icon on the **Modify** toolbar.
- Specify the base and destination points, as shown.

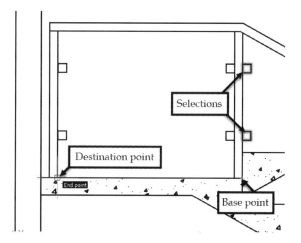

- Click the **Line** icon on the **Draw** toolbar. Next, select the corner points of the top and bottom steps, as shown.
- Press Esc.
- Select the newly created line and click the **Offset** icon on the **Modify** toolbar.
- Type 1" and press ENTER. Move the pointer upward and click.

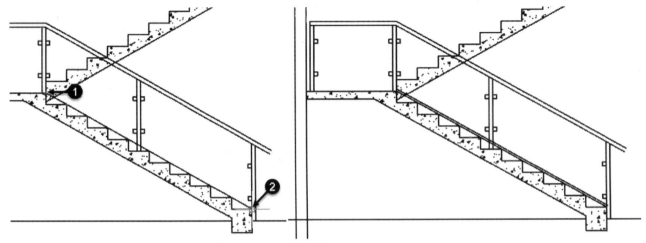

- Press ENTER twice. Next, type 2" and press ENTER.
- Select the newly offset line. Next, move the pointer upward and click.

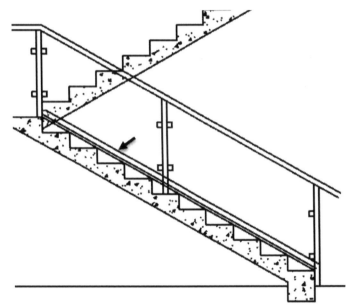

- On the menu bar, click **Modify > Trim Vectors**. Press ENTER.
- Trim the intersecting portions of the lines, as shown. Press Esc.

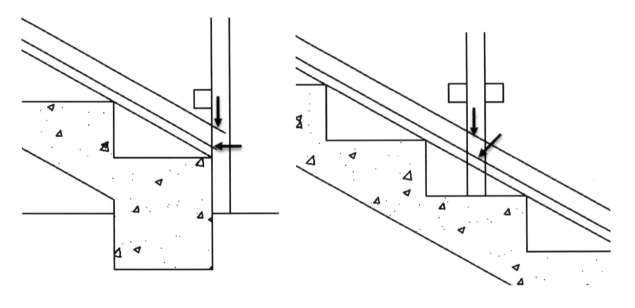

- Press and hold the SHIFT key and select the rectangles.
- Click **Move** on the **Modify** toolbar. Next, specify the base point, as shown.
- Move the pointer upward. Next, type 4" and press ENTER.

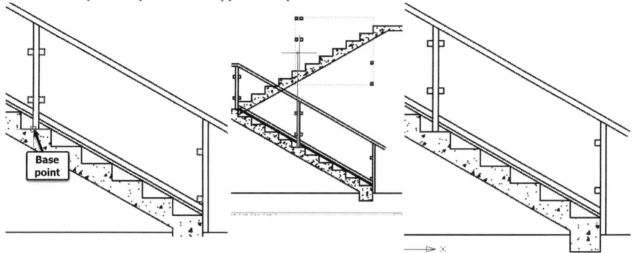

- Select the horizontal line, as shown. Next, click the **Offset** icon on the **Modify** toolbar.
- Type 33" and press ENTER. Next, move the pointer downward and click.
- Press ENTER twice. Next, type 2" and press ENTER.
- Select the newly offset line. Next, move the pointer upward and click.

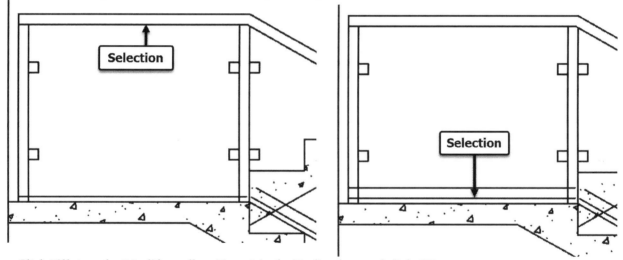

- Click **Fillet** on the **Modify** toolbar. Type **0** in the **Radius** box and click **OK**.
- Select the horizontal and inclined lines, as shown.
- Press ENTER and select the horizontal and inclined lines, as shown.

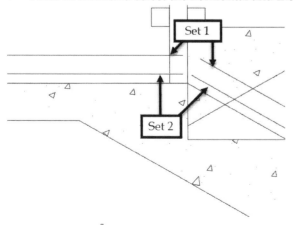

- Click **Trim Vectors** on the **Modify** toolbar. Next, press ENTER.
- Select the portions of the horizontal and inclined line, as shown.

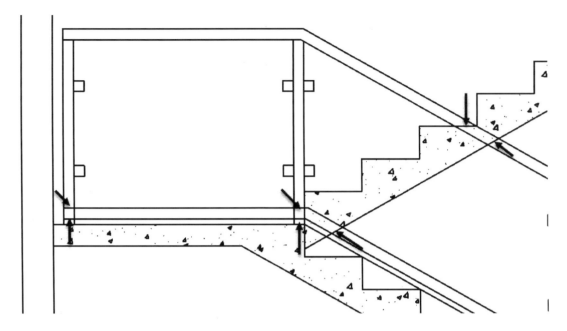

- Right-click and select the **eRase** option.
- Press and hold the SHIFT key and select the inclined lines, as shown. Next, press ENTER.

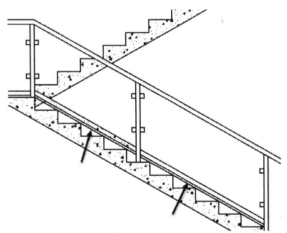

- Close the end of the offset lines using the **Line** tool.

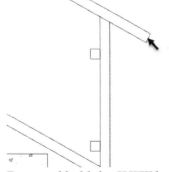

- Press and hold the SHIFT key and select the elements of the handrail.

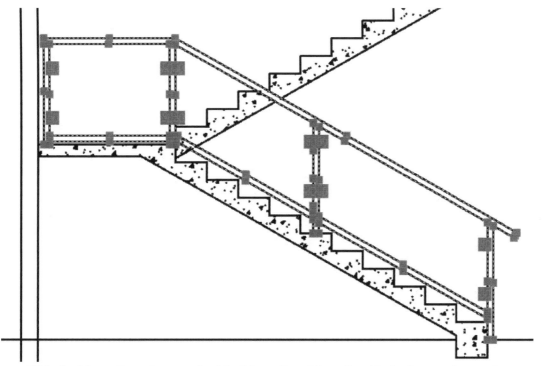

- Click the **Move Copy** icon on the **Modify** toolbar. Next, Specify the base point, as shown.
- Move the pointer toward the right and click to create the copy.

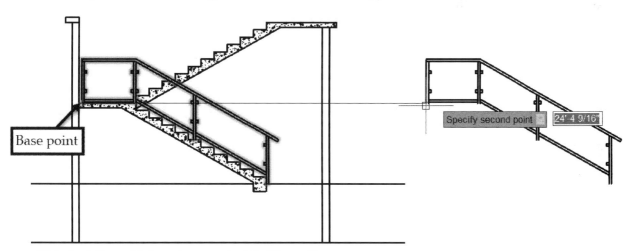

- Click the **Mirror Objects** icon on the **Modify** toolbar.
- Create a selection window covering all the copied entities of the handrail. Next, press ENTER.
- Select the base point, as shown. Next, move the pointer vertically upward and click. Next, select **Yes**.

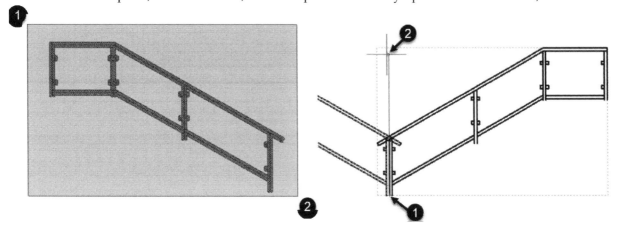

- Create a selection window across all the mirrored entities.
- Click the **Move** icon on the **Modify** toolbar. Next, specify the base point, as shown.
- Move the pointer toward the right and select the destination point.

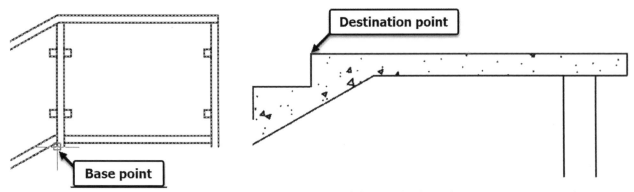

- Press and hold the SHIFT key and select the elements of the handrail, as shown. Next, press Delete.

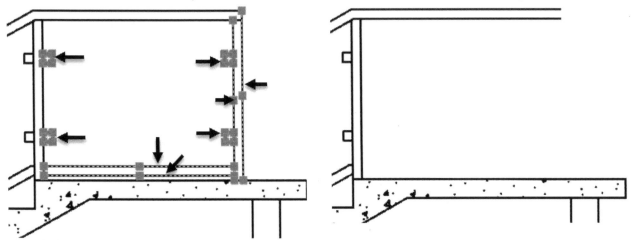

- Click the **Line** icon on the **Draw** toolbar. Next, select the endpoint of the vertical line, as shown.
- Move the pointer upward, type 2, and then press ENTER.

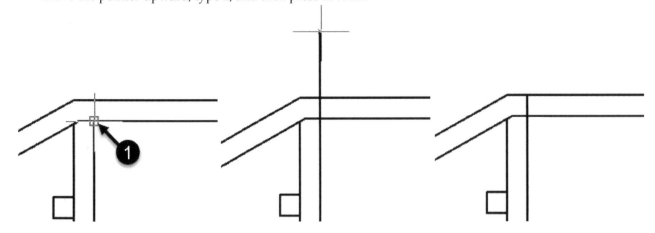

- Select the newly created line. Next, click on the midpoint of the selected line.
- Move the pointer toward the right. Type 12 and press ENTER.

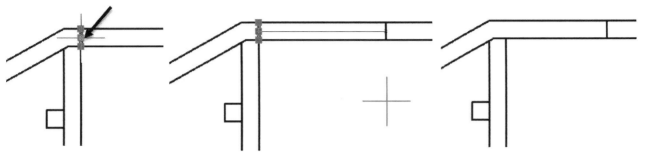

- Click the **Trim Vectors** icon on the **Modify** toolbar. Next, press ENTER.
- Trim the unwanted elements.

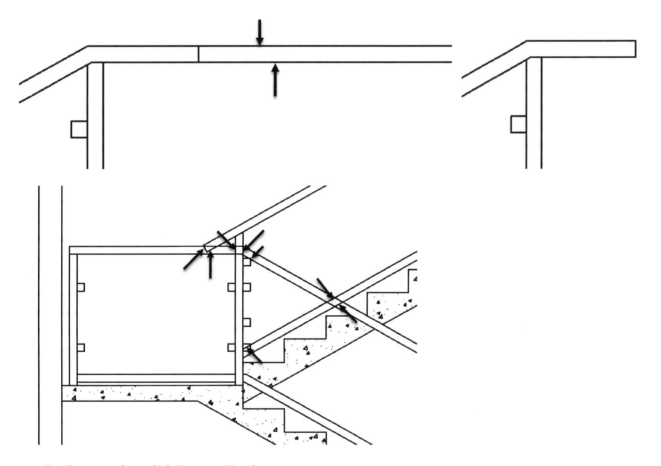

- On the menu bar, click **Draw > Hatch**.
- On the **Hatch** dialog, click the **Patterns** [ ] icon next to the **Pattern** drop-down,
- Click the **Other Predefined** tab on the **Hatch Pattern** dialog, and then select the **DOTS** pattern.
- Click **OK** on the **Hatch Pattern** dialog.
- Click the **Add: Pick points** icon under the **Boundary** section. Next, pick points in the areas, as shown.

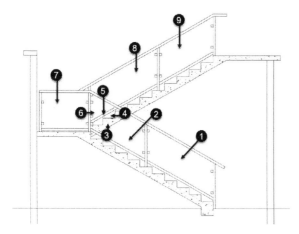

- Press ENTER.
- Type **2** in the **Scale** box under the **Angle and Scale** section and click **OK** on the **Hatch** dialog.

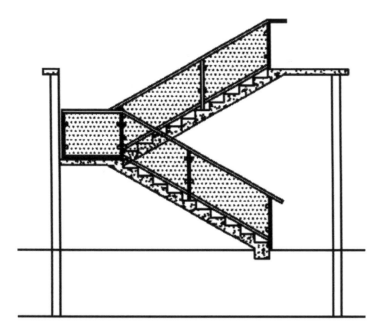

- Delete the construction lines, as shown.

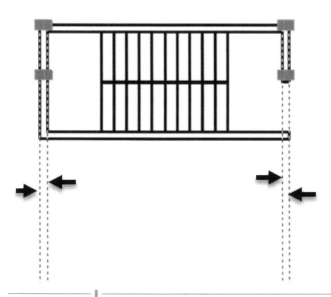

- Save and close the file.

Tutorial 3: Creating the Elevation View

In this tutorial, you will create the elevation view using the floor plan.

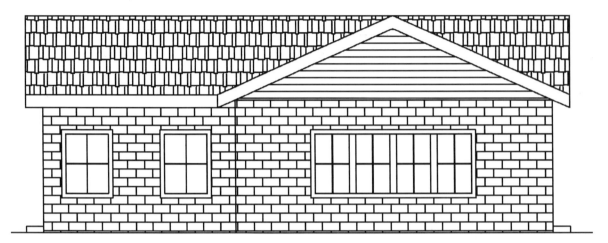

- Download the Elevation_plan from the companion website and open it.
- Click the **Layer Manager Dialog** icon on the **Properties** toolbar.
- Click the **Add** icon on the **Layers** dialog. Next, type Elevation as the layer name.
- Double-click on the Elevation layer. Next, close the **Layers** dialog.

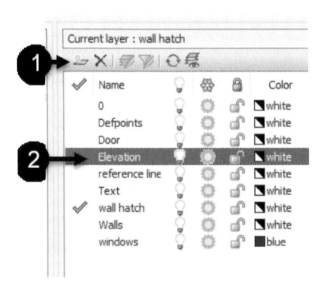

- Draw a horizontal line above the floor plan, as shown.

- On the menu bar, click **Draw > Ray**.
- Select the top-left corner of the floor plan. Next, move the pointer upward and click.

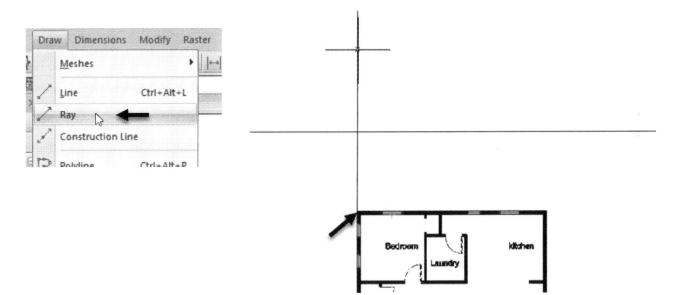

- Press ENTER twice.
- Select the top-right corner of the floor plan. Next, move the pointer upward and click.

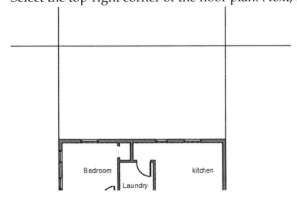

- Click the **Offset** tool on the **Modify** toolbar.
- Type 6" and press ENTER. Next, select the horizontal line.
- Move the pointer upward and click to create an offset line. Next, press ENTER twice.
- Type 9' as the offset distance. Next, press ENTER.
- Select the offset line created previously. Move the pointer upward and click.

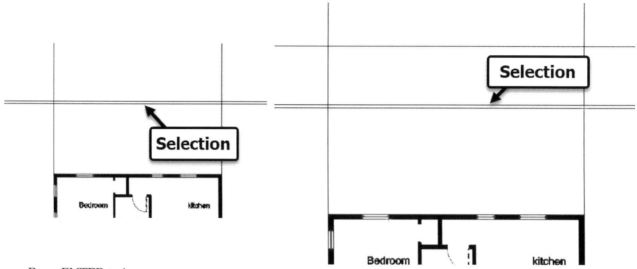

- Press ENTER twice.
- Type 10′ as the offset distance. Next, press ENTER.
- Select the offset line created previously. Next, move the pointer upward and click.
- Press ENTER twice.
- Type 6′ as the offset distance. Next, press ENTER.
- Select the offset line created previously. Move the pointer upward and click.

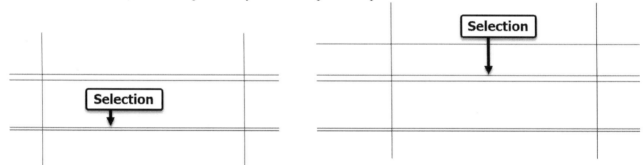

- On the menu bar, click **Draw > Construction Line**.
- Right click and select the **Offset** option from the shortcut menu.
- Type 16″ as the offset distance. Next, press ENTER.
- Select the right exterior wall. Next, move the pointer toward the right and click.
- Select the left exterior wall. Move the pointer toward the left and click.

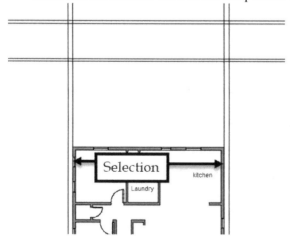

- Press ENTER twice.
- Right click and select the **Ver** option.

- Select the corner point of the exterior wall, as shown.
- Press ENTER twice.
- Right click and select the **Offset** option from the shortcut menu.
- Type 16" as the offset distance. Next, press ENTER.
- Select the construction line created in the last step. Next, move the pointer toward the left and click.

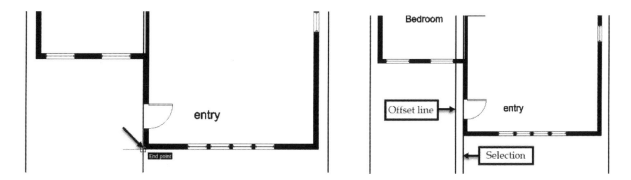

- On the menu bar, click **Modify > Break Vectors at Point** .
- Select the horizontal line, as shown.
- Select the intersection point between the horizontal and vertical lines, as shown.

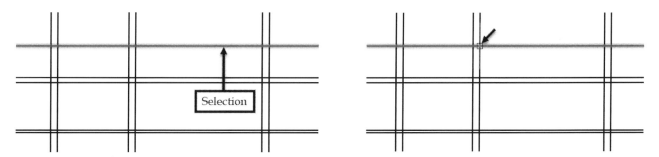

- Press ENTER to activate the **Break Vectors at Point** tool.
- Select the right portion of the broken line.
- Select the intersection point between the horizontal and vertical lines, as shown.

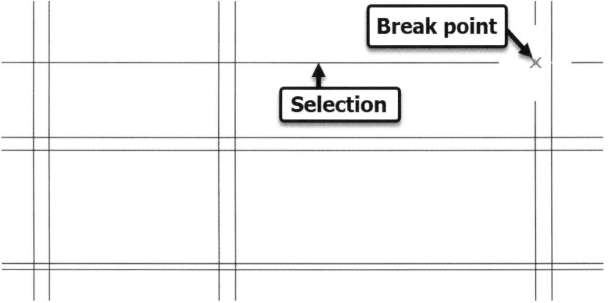

- Click the **Line** tool on the **Draw** toolbar.
- Select the midpoint of the broken line, as shown.

- Select the intersection point between the horizontal and vertical lines, as shown.

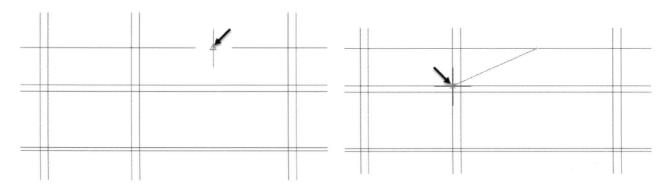

- Press ENTER twice. Next, select the start point of the line created in the last step.
- Select the intersection point between the horizontal and vertical lines, as shown.

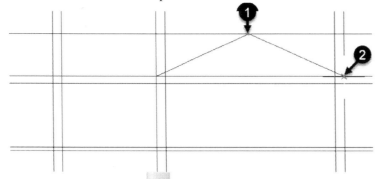

- Click **Trim Vectors** ⊬ on the **Modify** toolbar. Next, press ENTER.
- Select the portions of the vertical lines, as shown.

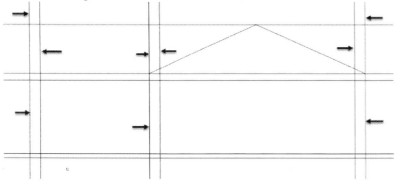

- Select the **eRase** option from the command line.
- Click and drag the mouse pointer across the vertical lines, as shown.
- Press ENTER twice and drag a selection window across the vertical lines, as shown.

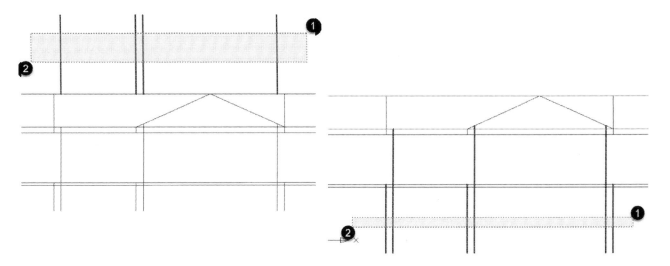

- Trim the horizontal and vertical lines, as shown.

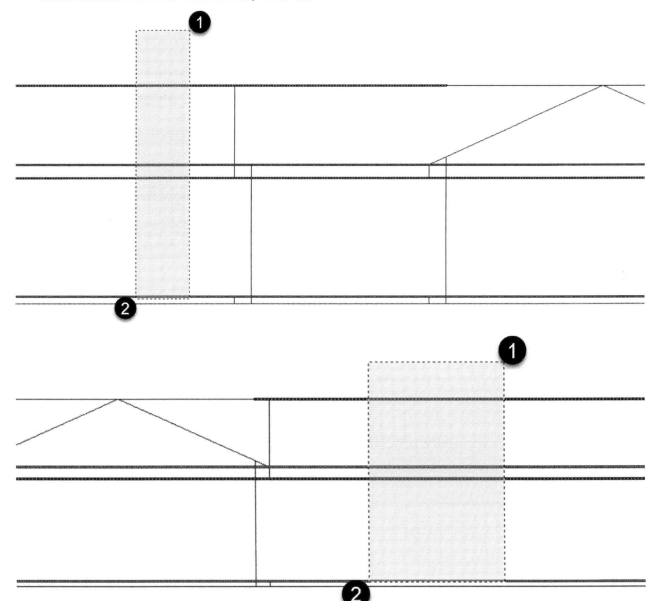

- Trim the small portions, as shown.

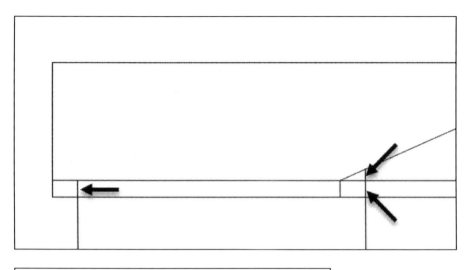

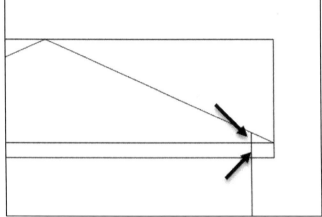

- Press Esc. Next, select the inclined line, as shown.
- Click the **Move Copy** tool on the **Modify** toolbar. Next, specify the base point, as shown.
- Move the pointer downward and select the intersection point, as shown.

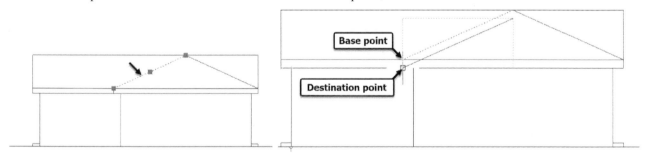

- Press Esc.
- Likewise, copy the other inclined line, as shown.

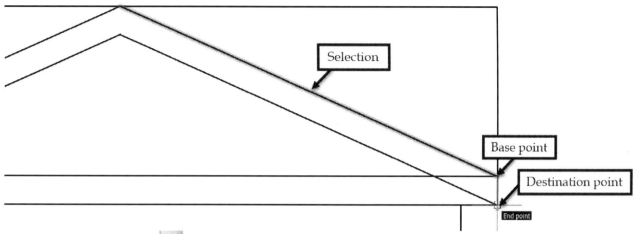

- Click the **Trim Vectors** 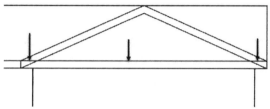 icon on the **Modify** toolbar. Next, press ENTER.
- Select the portions of the horizontal line, as shown.

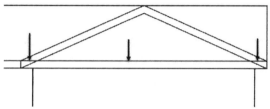

- On the menu bar, click **Modify > Break Vectors at Point**.
- Select the horizontal line, as shown. Next, select the intersection point, as shown.
- On the menu bar, click **Modify > Break Vectors at Point**.
- Select the vertical line, as shown. Next, select the intersection point, as shown.

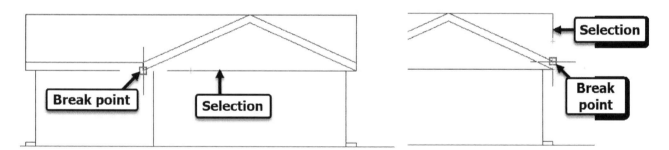

- On the menu bar, click **Modify > Break Vectors at Point**.
- Select the vertical line, as shown. Next, select the intersection point, as shown.
- Select the horizontal line, as shown. Next, press Delete.

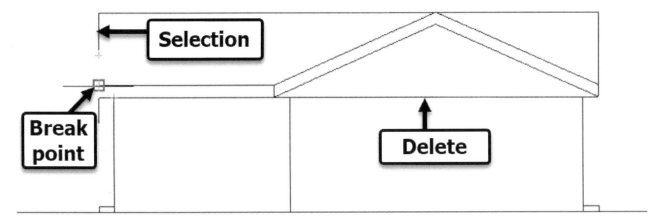

- Click the **Extend Vectors** icon on the **Modify** toolbar. Next, press ENTER.
- Select the two vertical lines, as shown.

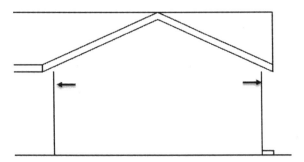

- Create a horizontal line connecting the endpoints of the two vertical lines.
- Select the two construction lines, as shown.
- Press Delete.

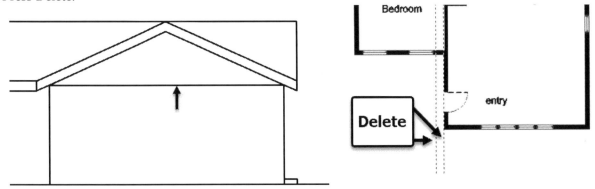

- On the menu bar, click **Draw > Construction Line** tool.
- Right-click and select the **Ver** option.
- Zoom to the lower portion of the floor plan and select the vertex points on the window, as shown.

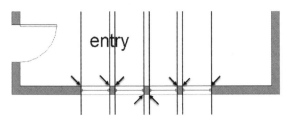

- Click the **Offset** tool on the **Modify** toolbar.
- Type 3′ as the offset distance. Next, press ENTER.
- Select the horizontal line, as shown. Next, move the pointer upward and click.

- Click the **Draw > Rectangle by > Two Points** on the menu bar.
- Select the intersection point, as shown.

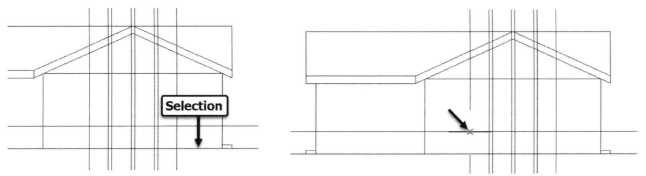

- Right-click and select the **Dimensions** option.
- Select the two intersection points, as shown.
- Type 54 as the rectangle width and press ENTER. Next, move the pointer upward and click.

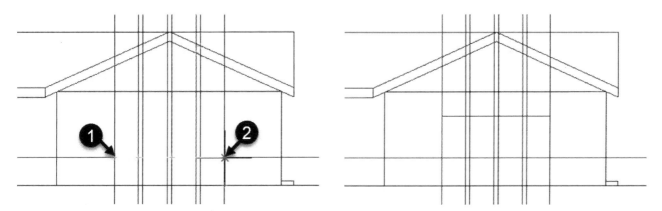

- Click the **Offset** tool on the **Modify** toolbar.
- Type 4" as the offset distance. Next, press ENTER.
- Select the rectangle. Next, move the pointer outward and click.

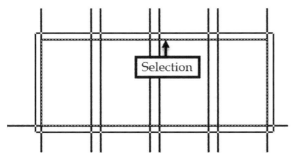

- Click the **Trim Vectors** icon on the **Modify** toolbar. Next, press ENTER.
- Click and drag the pointer across the vertical lines, as shown.

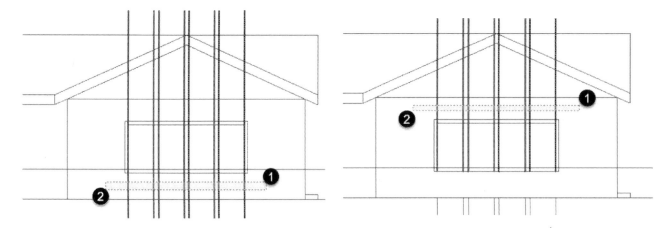

- Select the portions of the vertical lines, as shown.

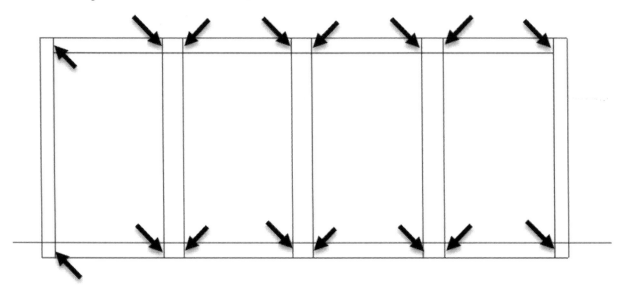

- Press ENTER.
- Press and hold the SHIFT key and select the vertical and horizontal construction lines. Next, press Delete.

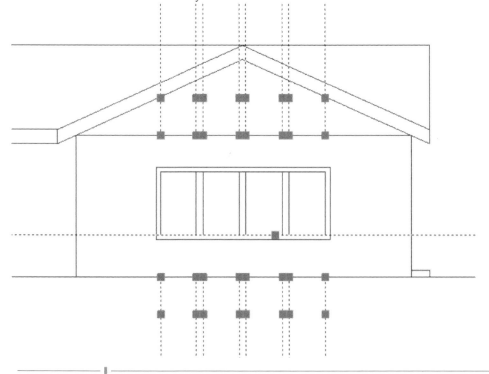

- Select the two rectangles and click the **Explode** ⬤ tool on the **Modify** panel of the **Home** menu bar tab.

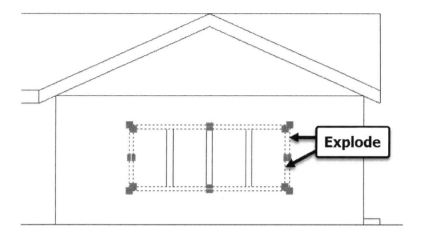

- On the menu bar, click **Draw > Line**. Next, select the midpoint of the left vertical line, as shown.
- Move the pointer toward the right and select the midpoint of the right vertical line, as shown.
- Press ESC.

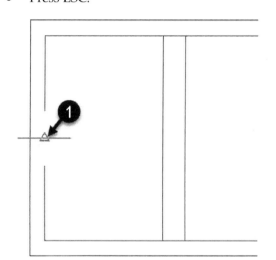
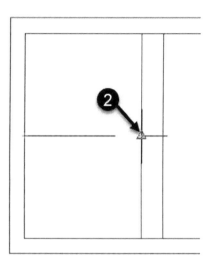

- Click the **Offset** icon on the **Modify** toolbar. Next, the endpoint and the midpoint of the newly created horizontal line.
- Select the right vertical line and click on the left side of the selected line.

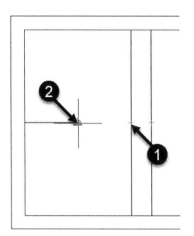
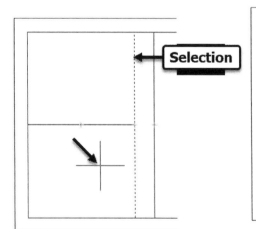
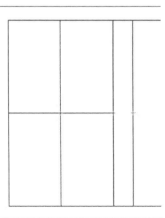

- Click the **Move Copy** ![icon] tool on the **Modify** toolbar.
- Press and hold the SHIFT key and select the newly created lines. Next, press ENTER.
- Select the lower-left corner point.
- Move the pointer toward the right and select the corner point, as shown.
- Likewise, create two more copies of the multi-lines, as shown.
  +`

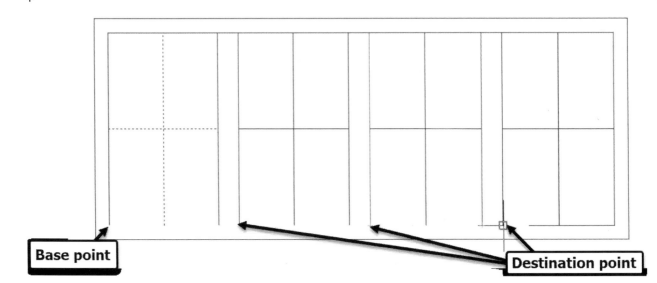

Base point

Destination point

- Likewise, create two windows on the left side.
- Delete the construction lines.

- Click the **Add Hatch** ![icon] tool on the **Draw** toolbar.

- On the **Hatch** dialog, click the **Patterns** ![icon] icon next to the **Pattern** drop-down,
- Click the **Other Predefined** tab on the **Hatch Pattern** dialog, and then select the **AR-RSHKE** pattern.
- Click **OK** on the **Hatch Pattern** dialog.
- Click the **Add: Pick points** icon under the **Boundary** section. Next, pick points in the areas, as shown.

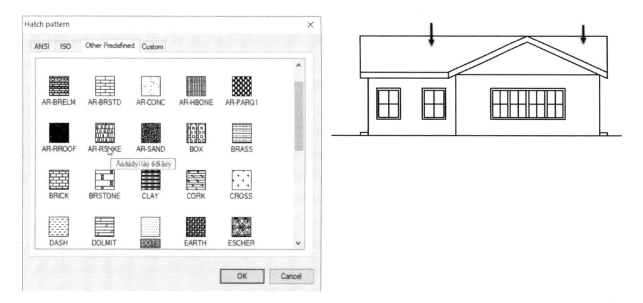

- Press ENTER.
- Type **1** in the **Scale** box under the **Angle and Scale** section and click **OK** on the **Hatch** dialog.
- Click the **Add Hatch** tool on the **Draw** toolbar.
- On the **Hatch** dialog, click the **Patterns** icon next to the **Pattern** drop-down,
- Click the **Other Predefined** tab on the **Hatch Pattern** dialog, and then select the **AR-B816** pattern.
- Click **OK** on the **Hatch Pattern** dialog.
- Click the **Add: Pick points** icon under the **Boundary** section. Next, pick points in the areas, as shown.

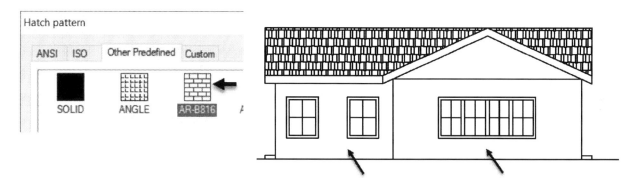

- Press ENTER.
- Click the **Additional Options** button on the bottom right corner of the **Hatch** dialog.
- Select the **Outer** option from the **Islands** section. Next, click **OK**.

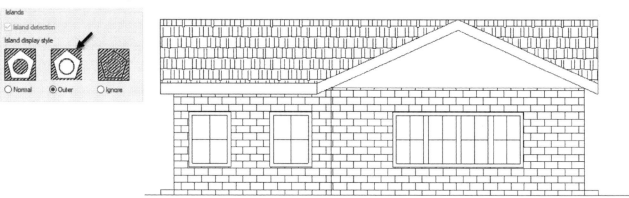

- Click the **Add Hatch**  tool on the **Draw** toolbar.

- On the **Hatch** dialog, click the **Patterns**  icon next to the **Pattern** drop-down,
- Click the **ANSI** tab on the **Hatch Pattern** dialog, and then select the **ANSI31** pattern.
- Click **OK** on the **Hatch Pattern** dialog.
- Click the **Add: Pick points** icon under the **Boundary** section. Next, pick points in the areas, as shown.
- Press ENTER.
- Enter **135** and **50** in the **Angle** and **Scale** boxes, respectively. Click **OK**.

- Save and close the file.

Tutorial 4: Creating the Roof Plan

In this tutorial, you will create the Roof plan using the floor plan.

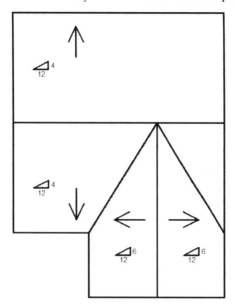

- Download the Floor_plan.dwg from the companion website.
- Click the **New document** icon on the **Main** toolbar.

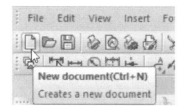

- On the menu bar, click the **Format > Units**. The **Drawing Units** dialog appears.
- On the **Drawing Units** dialog, select **Type > Architectural** from the **Length** section.
- Select **Precision > 0-01/16**. Next, set the **Units to scale inserted content** to **Inches**, and click **OK**.
- Click the **Insert > DWG Reference** on the menu bar.
- On the **External Reference** dialog, go to the location of the Floor_plan.dwg file and double-click on it.
- Check the **Specify Later** option from the **Insertion Point** section.
- Click **OK** on the **External Reference** dialog. Next, click in the graphics window.
- Click **View > Zoom > Zoom All** on the menu bar.

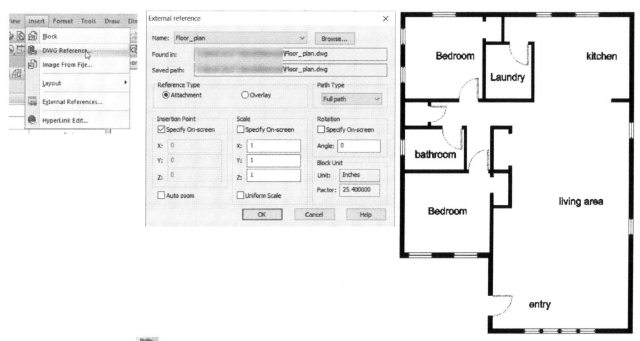

- Click the **Polyline** tool on the **Draw** toolbar.
- Select the corner points of the floor plan. Next, right-click and select the **Close** option.

- Select the drawing attachment and press DELETE.

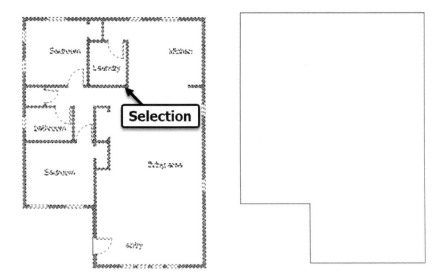

- Click the **Offset** tool on the **Modify** toolbar.
- Type 16 and press ENTER. Next, select the newly created polyline.
- Move the pointer outward and click.

- Click the **Erase** tool on the **Modify** toolbar.
- Select the polyline used to create the offset. Next, press ENTER.

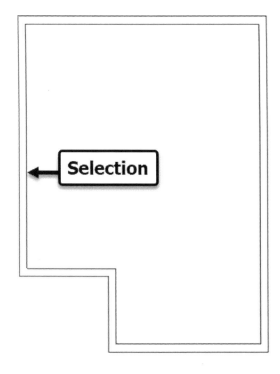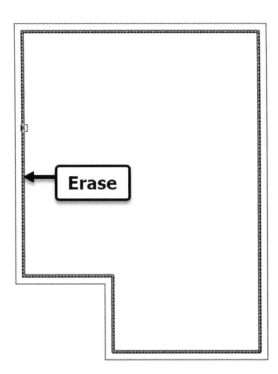

- Click the **Line** tool on the **Draw** toolbar. Next, select the midpoint of the left vertical line.
- Make sure the ORTHO button is active on the status bar.
- Move the pointer toward the right and click. Next, press ENTER twice.

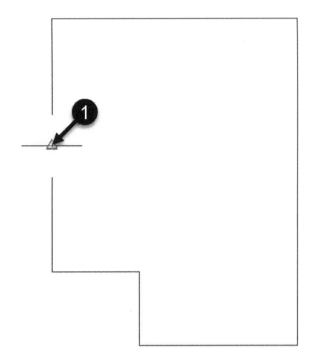
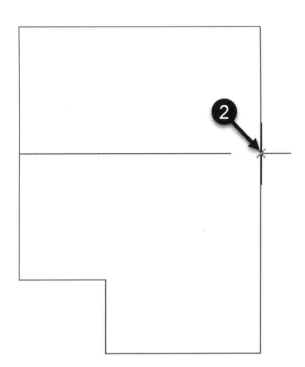

- Select the midpoint of the lower horizontal line, as shown.
- Move the pointer upward and click.

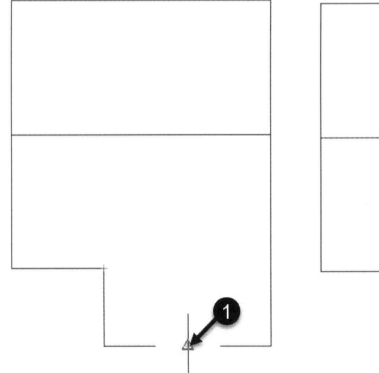
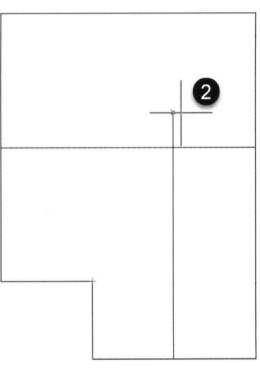

- Click the **Trim Vectors** on the **Modify** toolbar. Next, press ENTER.
- Select the unwanted portions of the line, as shown.

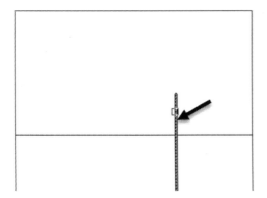

- Click the **Line** tool on the **Draw** toolbar. Next, select the corner point of the polyline.
- Select the intersection point of the vertical and horizontal lines. Next, press ESC.

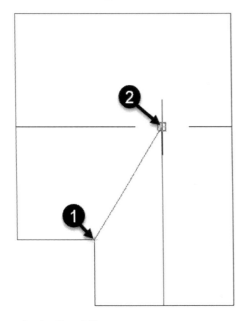

- Select the inclined line.

- Click the **Mirror** tool on the **Modify** toolbar.
- Select the endpoints of the vertical line. Next, select the **No** option from the command line.

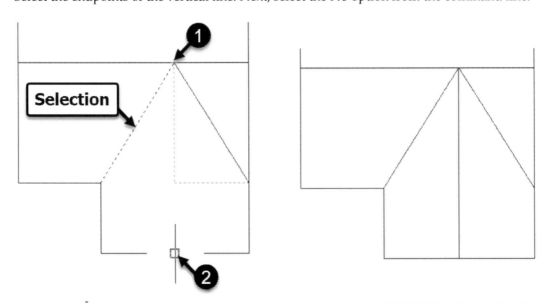

- Click the **Line** tool on the **Draw** toolbar. Next, click in the graphics window.
- Move the pointer toward the right. Next, type 36 and press ENTER.
- Move the pointer upward. Next, type 18 and press ENTER.
- Select the start point of the horizontal line.

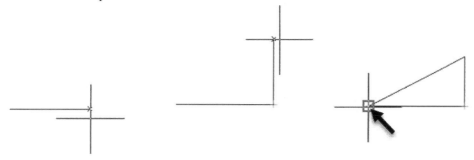

- Click **Draw > Text > Single Line Text** on the menu bar. Next, click in the graphics window.

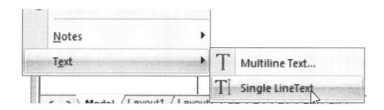

- Type **12** as the text height. Next, press ENTER. Next, type 0 as the rotation angle, and then press ENTER.
- Type 4 and click in the graphics window.
- Type 12 and click in the graphics window. Next, press ESC.
- Select the 4 text and click on its base point. Next, move the pointer and click at the location, as shown.
- Likewise, position the 12 text at the location, as shown.

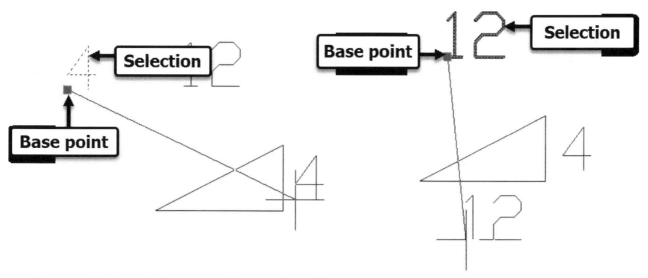

- Create a selection window across the triangle and the texts.
- Click the **Move Copy** tool on the **Modify** toolbar. Next, select the base point, as shown.

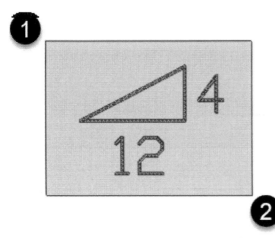

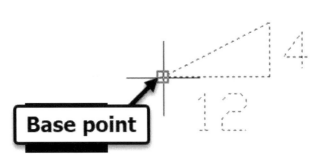

- Place the copies at the locations, as shown.

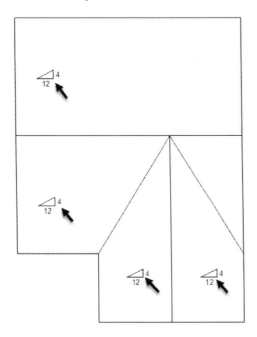

- Zoom the lower portion of the drawing. Next, double-click on 4.
- Type **6** in the **Text** box and click **OK**.
- Likewise, change the text on the right side to 6. Next, press ESC.

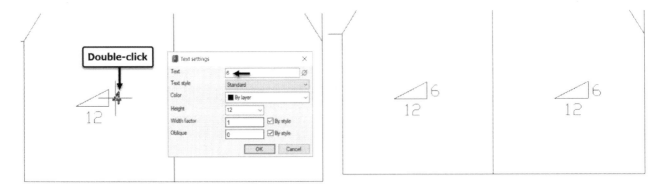

- Click **Draw > Rectangle by > Two Points** on the menu bar.

- Click at the location, as shown. Next, right-click and select the **Dimensions** option.
- Type 36 and press ENTER.

- Type -72 and press ENTER. Next, click on the right side.

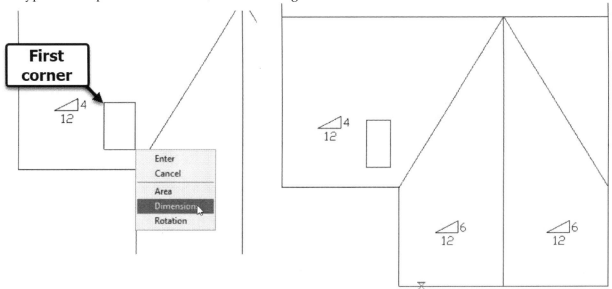

- Click the **Line** tool on the **Draw** toolbar.
- Select the midpoints of the horizontal edges of the rectangle.

- Press ENTER twice. Next, select the midpoint of the left vertical edge of the rectangle.
- Select the lower endpoint of the vertical line. Next, select the midpoint of the right vertical edge of the rectangle.

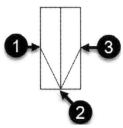

- Press ESC.
- Select the rectangle and press Delete.

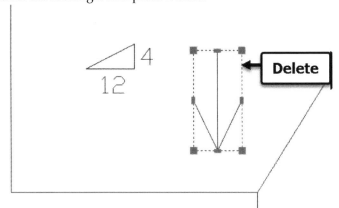

- Create a selection window across all the elements of the arrow.

- Click the **Mirror** icon on the **Modify** toolbar.
- Select the endpoints of the horizontal line to define the mirror line. Next, right-click and select **NO**.

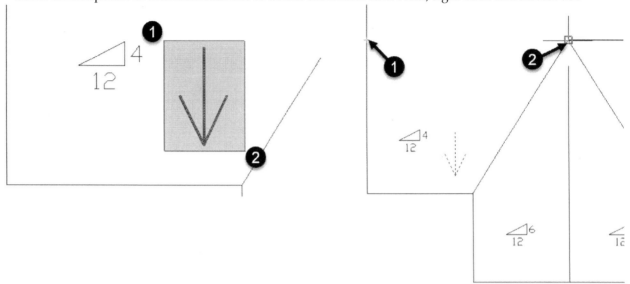

- Create a selection window across all the elements of the arrow.
- Click the **Rotate** tool on the **Modify** toolbar.
- Select the base point, as shown.
- Right-click and select the **Copy** option.
- Move the pointer vertically downward and click.

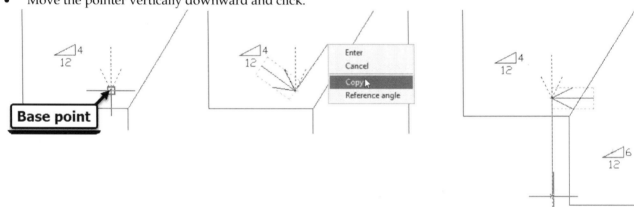

- Press and hold the SHIFT key and select the elements of the rotated arrow.
- Click the **Move** tool on the **Modify** toolbar.
- Select the base point, as shown. Next, move the pointer toward the right and click.

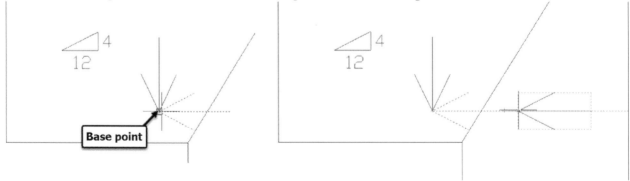

- Select the elements of the arrow moving in the previous step.
- Click the **Mirror** tool on the **Modify** toolbar.
- Select the endpoints of the vertical line, as shown.

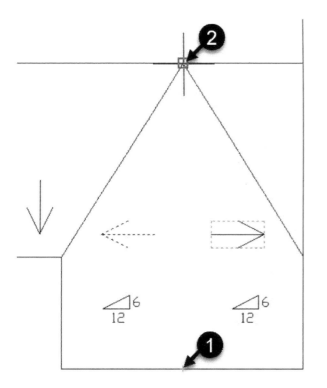
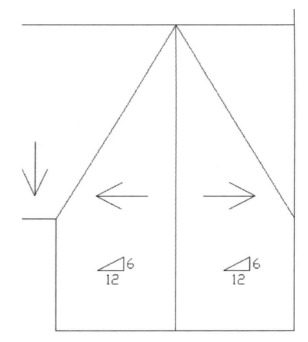

- Right-click and select **No**.
- Save and close the drawing file.

Tutorial 5: Creating the Wall and Roof Detail

In this tutorial, you will create the Roof and wall detail.

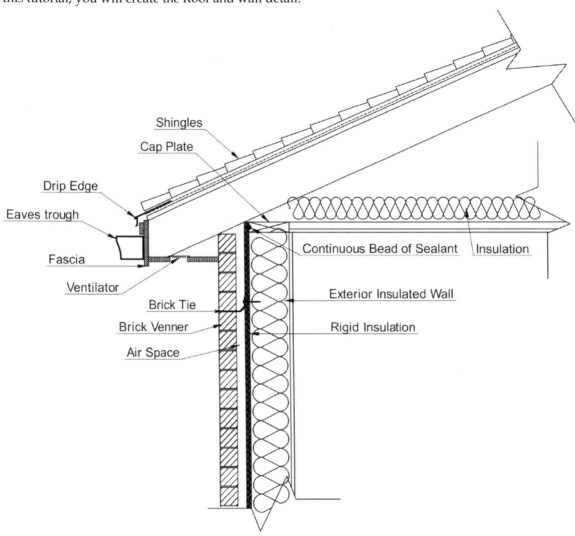

- Download the Roof_&_wall_detail.dwg file and open it.
- Click the **Layers Manager Dialog** tool on the **Properties** toolbar.
- Create a new layer and name it Roof_wall_detail. Next, make the new layer are current.

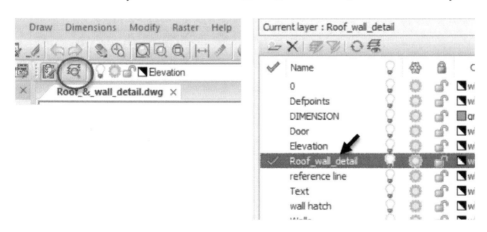

- Close the **Layers** dialog.
- On the menu bar, click > **Draw** > **Ray** tool.

- Create the projection lines from the elevation view, as shown.
- Create a vertical line, as shown.

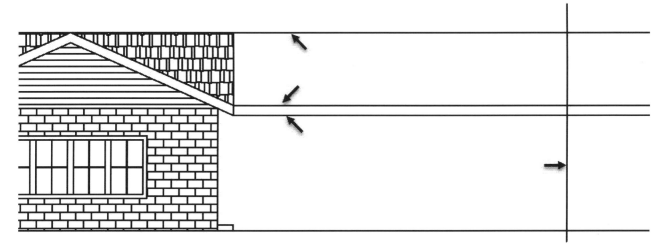

- Select the two inclined lines of the roof, as shown.
- Select the two vertical lines, as shown.

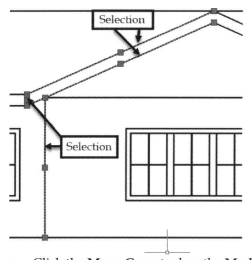

- Click the **Move Copy** tool on the **Modify** toolbar. Next, select the base point, as shown.
- Move the pointer toward the right and select the intersection point, as shown.

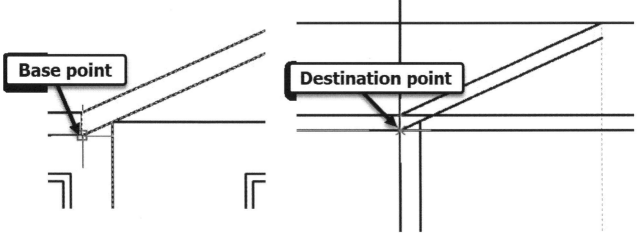

- Delete the reference lines, as shown.
- Click the **Trim Vectors** icon on the **Modify** toolbar. Next, press ENTER.
- Select the portion of the horizontal line, as shown.

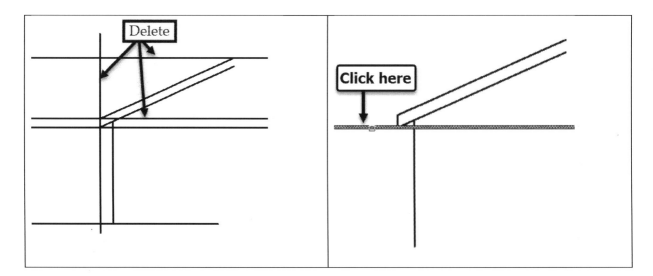

- Click the **Offset** tool on the **Modify** toolbar. Next, type 4 and press ENTER.
- Select the vertical line. Next, move the pointer toward the right and click.
- Press ENTER twice. Next, type 2 and press ENTER.
- Select the offset line. Next, move the pointer toward the right and click.

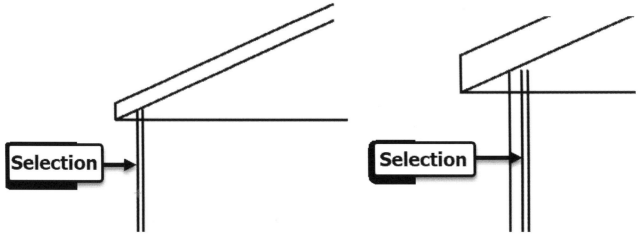

Creating the Brick Veneer

- Click the **Draw > Rectangle by > Two points** on the menu bar.
- Specify the corner point, as shown.
- Right-click and select the **Dimensions** option. Next, type 4 and press ENTER.
- Type 4 and press ENTER.

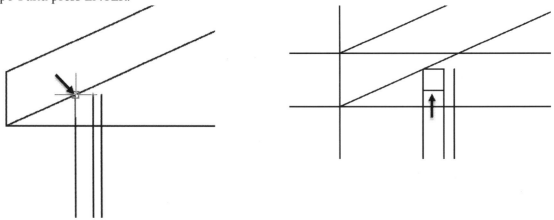

- Click the **Line** tool on the **Draw** toolbar. Next, zoom to the top portion of the drawing.
- Select the lower-left corner of the rectangle. Move the pointer downward and type 0.25. Next, press ENTER twice.
- Select the newly created line.
- Click the **Move** tool on the **Modify** toolbar.
- Select the top endpoint of the selected line. Next, move the pointer toward the right.
- Type 0.125, and press ENTER.

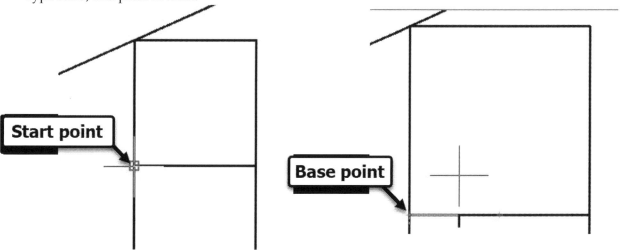

- Select the line moved in the last step. Next, click the **Offset** icon on the **Modify** toolbar.
- Type **3.75** and press ENTER. Next, click on the right side.

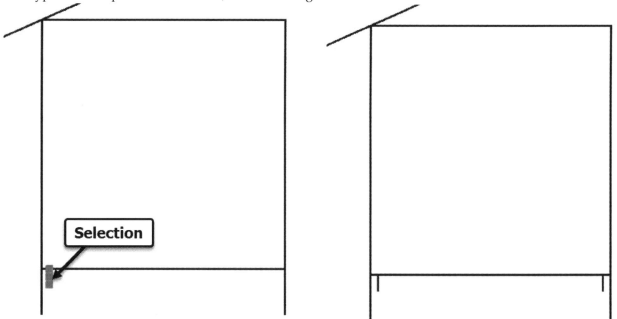

- Select the rectangle and two lines. Next, click the **2D array** icon on the **Modify** toolbar.
- Select the **Rectangular Array** option from the **Array** dialog.
- Type 14 and 1 in the **Row** and **Column** boxes, respectively.
- Type -**4.25** in the **Row Offset** box. Next, press ENTER.

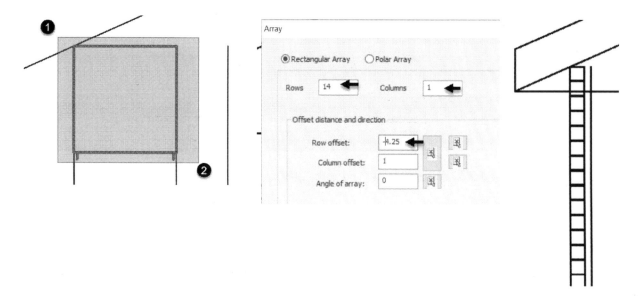

- Create a selection window across all the rectangles.
- Click the **Explode** tool on the **Modify** toolbar. All the rectangles are exploded into individual objects.

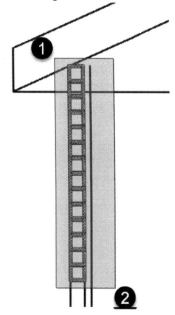

- Select the two vertical lines, as shown. Next, press Delete.

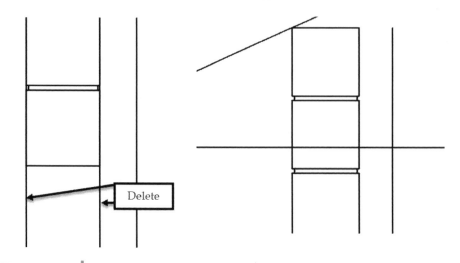

- Click the **Add Hatch** 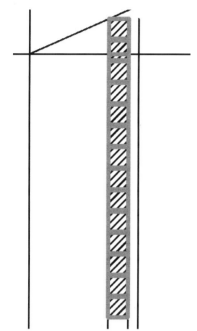 tool on the **Draw** toolbar.
- Select the **ANSI31** pattern from the **Pattern** drop-down.
- Type 8 in the **Scale** box in the **Angle and Scale** section.
- Click the **Add: Pick points** icon in the **Boundaries** section and click in the regions, as shown.

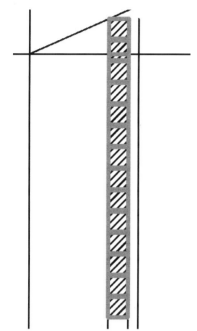

- Press and ENTER.

Creating the Brick Tie

- On the menu bar, click **View** > **Zoom** drop-down > **Zoom Window** 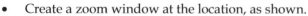.
- Create a zoom window at the location, as shown.

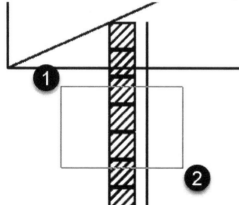

- Click the **Offset** tool on the **Modify** toolbar.
- Type 0.025, and press ENTER. Next, offset the two horizontal lines in the inward direction.

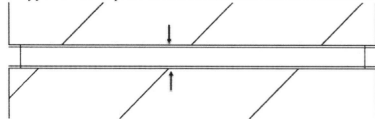

- Press ENTER twice.

- Type 1 and press ENTER. Next, offset the left vertical line towards the right.

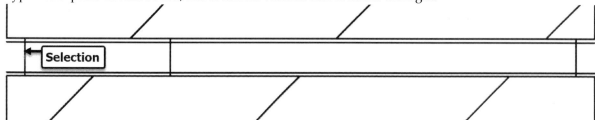

- Click the **Trim Vectors** icon on the **Modify** toolbar. Next, press ENTER.
- Trim the portions of the lines, as shown.

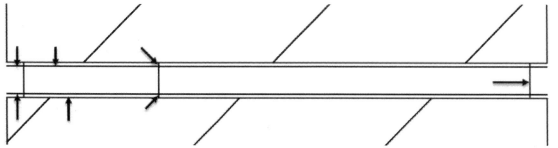

- Click the **Extend Vectors** icon on the **Modify** toolbar. Next, press ENTER.
- Select the ends of the horizontal lines, as shown. The horizontal lines are extended up to the right vertical line.

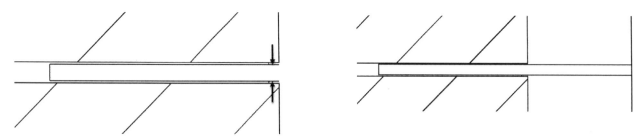

- Click the **Line** tool on the **Draw** toolbar.
- Select the endpoint of the lower horizontal line. Next, move the pointer vertically upward.
- Type 3 and press ENTER.
- Click the **Offset** tool on the **Modify** toolbar. Next, type 0.2 and press ENTER.
- Select the vertical line created in the last step.
- Move the pointer toward the left and click.

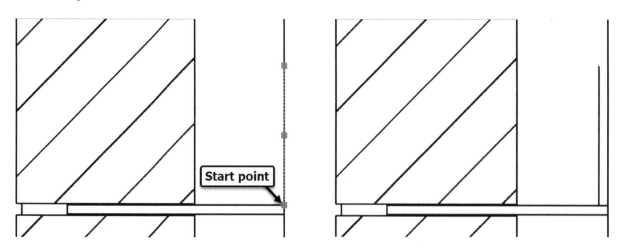

- Click the **Chamfer** on the **Modify** toolbar.
- Type 1 in **Length 1** box and click **OK**.

- Type 45 as the chamfer angle. Next, select horizontal and vertical lines, as shown.
- Likewise, create another chamfer, as shown.
- Click the **Line** tool on the **Draw** toolbar. Next, cap the ends of the offset lines, as shown.

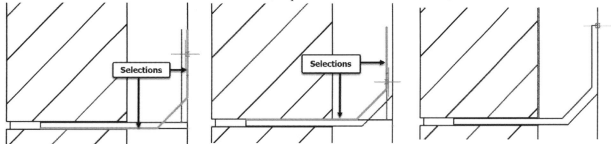

- Click **Draw > Rectangle by > Two points** on the menu bar. Next, click in the graphic window.
- Right-click and select the **Dimensions** option. Next, type 0.2 and press ENTER.
- Type 0.5 and press ENTER.
- Select the rectangle and click the **Move** tool on the **Modify** toolbar.
- Select the midpoint of the right vertical edge of the rectangle.
- Move the pointer and select the midpoint of the vertical line, as shown.

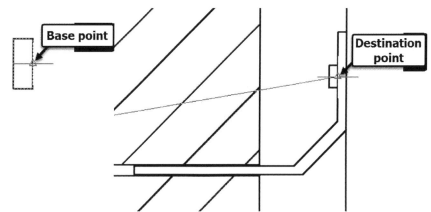

- Click the **Line** tool on the **Draw** toolbar.
- Select the midpoint of the right vertical edge of the rectangle. Next, move the pointer toward the right.
- Type 3.5 and press ENTER.
- Click the **Offset** tool on the **Modify** toolbar.
- Type 0.1 and press ENTER. Next, offset the newly created horizontal line on both sides.

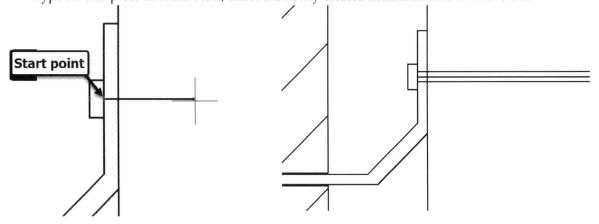

- Select the center line and press Delete.
- Click **Draw > Circle > Diameter** on the menu bar.

- Select the endpoints of the offset lines.

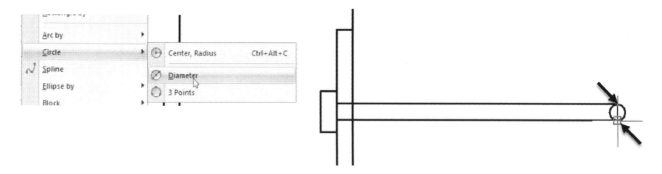

- Click the **Trim Vectors** tool on the **Modify** toolbar. Next, press ENTER.
- Select the unwanted portions, as shown.

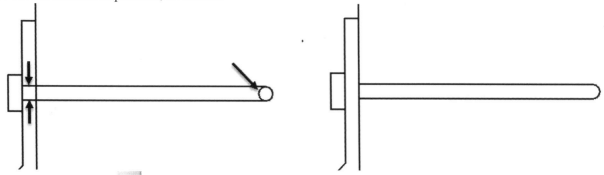

- Click the **Add Hatch** ⊞ tool on the **Draw** toolbar.
- Select the **SOLID** pattern from the **Pattern** drop-down.
- Click the **Add: Pick points** icon in the **Boundaries** section and click in the regions, as shown.
- Press ENTER and click **OK**.

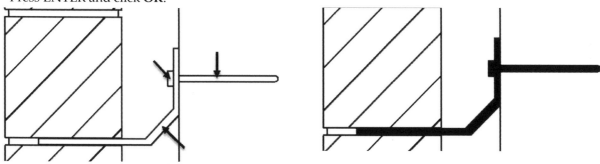

Creating the Insulation

- Click the **Offset** tool on the **Modify** toolbar. Next, type 1, and press ENTER.
- Select the vertical line, as shown. Next, move the pointer toward the right and click.
- Press ENTER twice. Next, type 9 and press ENTER.
- Select the offset line. Next, move the pointer toward the right and click.

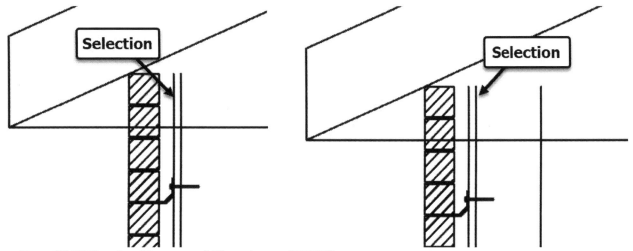

- Press ENTER twice. Next, type 0.75, and press ENTER.
- Select the offset line. Next, move the pointer toward the right and click.

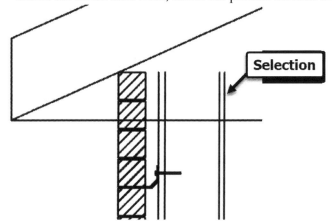

- Click the **Extend Vectors** icon on the **Modify** toolbar. Next, press ENTER.
- Click and drag a selection window across the ends of the vertical lines, as shown.
- Create the two horizontal lines, as shown.

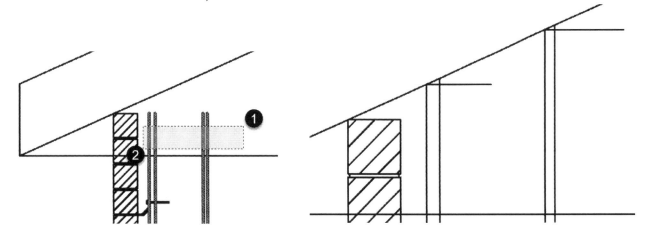

- Trim the extending portions.

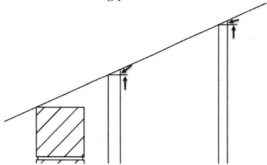

- Click the **Draw > Rectangle by > Two points** on the menu bar. Next, select the corner point, as shown.
- Right-click and select the **Dimensions** option. Next, type 9 and press ENTER.
- Type 2.25 and press ENTER. Move the pointer downward and click.

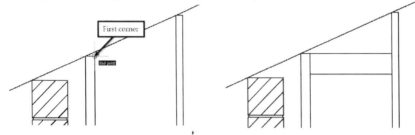

- Click the **Line** tool on the **Draw** toolbar.
- Create the diagonal lines by selecting the corner points of the rectangle.

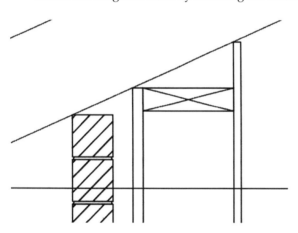

- Click **Draw > Circle** drop-down > **Circle, Radius** on the menu bar.
- Select the midpoint of the left vertical edge of the rectangle. Next, type 0.5, and press ENTER.

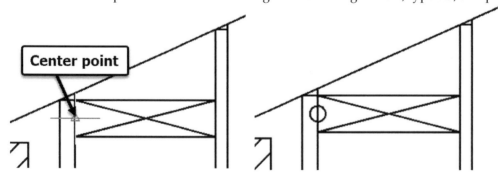

- Click the **Add Hatch** tool on the **Draw** toolbar.
- Select the **SOLID** pattern from the **Pattern** drop-down.

- Click the **Add: Select objects** 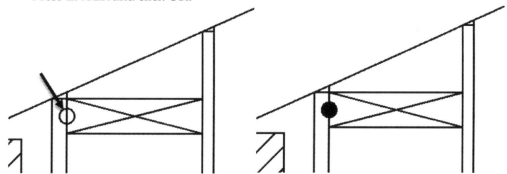 icon in the **Boundaries** section and select the circle, as shown.
- Press ENTER and click **OK**.

- Click the **Line** tool on the **Draw** toolbar. Next, create a horizontal line, as shown.
- Click the **Offset** tool on the **Modify** toolbar. Next, type 1.5 and press ENTER.
- Select the newly created line. Next, move the pointer downward and click.

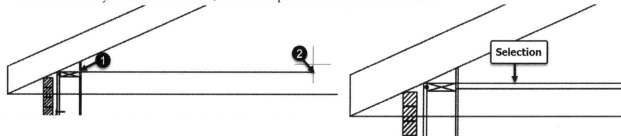

- Press ENTER twice. Next, type 0.75, and press ENTER.
- Select the offset line. Next, move the pointer downward and click.
- Click the **Trim Vectors** tool on the **Modify** toolbar.
- Trim the elements, as shown.

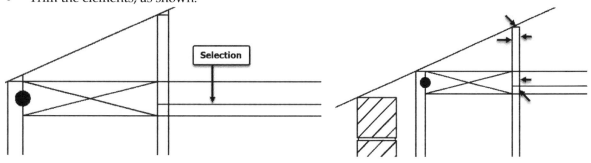

- Create a horizontal line, as shown.

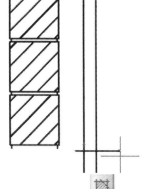

- Click the **Add Hatch** tool on the **Draw** toolbar.
- Select the **ANSI37** pattern from the **Pattern** drop-down.

- Type **2** in the **Scale** box. Next, type **45** in the **Angle** box.
- Click the **Add: Select objects** icon in the **Boundaries** section.
- Press and hold the SHIFT key and select the lines, as shown.
- Press ENTER and click **OK**.

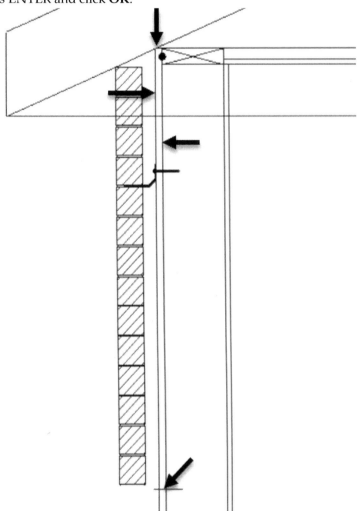

- Click the **Hatch** tool on the **Draw** panel of the **Home** menu bar tab.
- On the **Hatch /Fill** dialog, click the **Preview patterns** ⋯ icon next to the **Pattern** drop-down,
- Select the **ANSI** option from the **Select Pattern Style** dialog, and then select the **ANSI37** pattern. Next, click **OK**.
- Click the **Specify entities** icon and select the circle, as shown. Press ENTER and click **OK**.

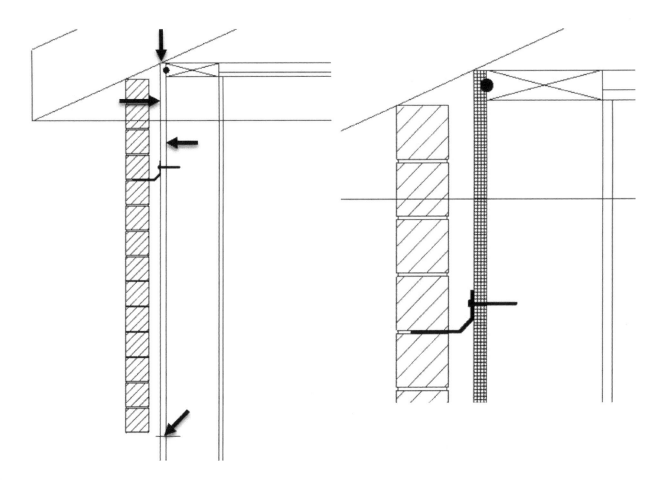

- Click the **Line** tool on the **Draw** toolbar.
- Select the midpoint of the horizontal line, as shown.
- Move the pointer downward and click. Next, press ESC.

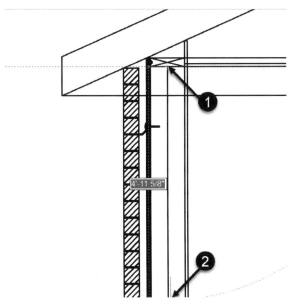

- On the menu bar, click **Format > Style**. Next, click the **Load linetypes** icon located at the top right corner of the dialog.
- Double-click on the ncad.in file. Next, select the **BATTING** linetype from the **Load Linetypes** dialog, and then click **OK**.
- Click **OK** on the **Linetype Manager** dialog.

- Click the **Layer Manager Dialog** icon on the **Properties** toolbar.
- Click the **Add** icon on the **Layers** dialog. Next, type **Insulation** as the layer name.
- Click in the **Line Type** column on the **Layers** dialog, and then select **BATTING**.

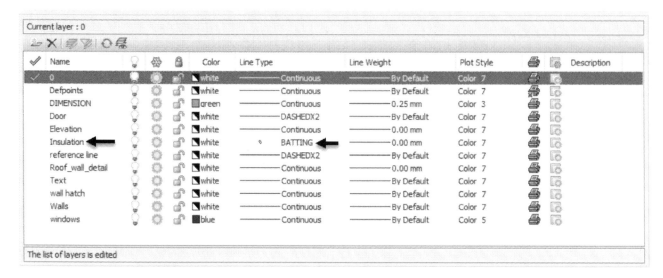

- Close the **Layers** dialog.
- Select the newly created line.
- Select **Insulation** from the **Layers** drop-down on the **Properties** toolbar.

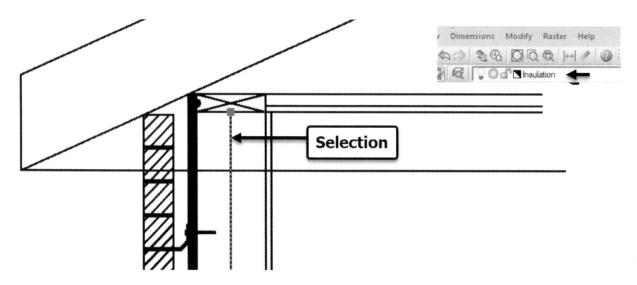

- Select the newly created line.
- Type 10 in the **Linetype Scale** box in the Inspector palette and press ENTER. Next, press ESC.

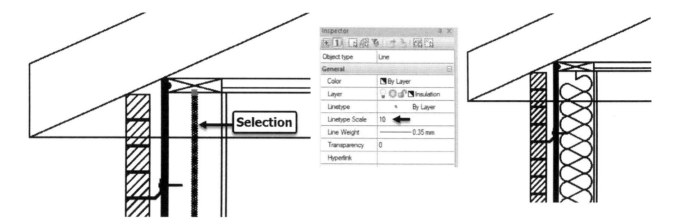

- Click the **Offset** tool on the **Modify** toolbar. Next, type 3 and press ENTER.
- Select the horizontal line, as shown. Next, move the pointer upward and click.

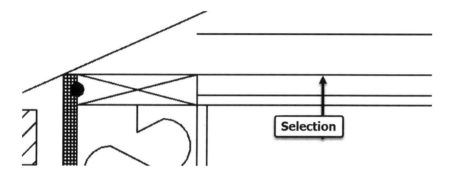

- Press ESC.
- Select the newly created line. Next, select **Insulation** from the **Layers** drop-down on the **Properties** toolbar.
- Type 6 in the **Linetype Scale** box in the Inspector palette and press ENTER. Next, press ESC.
- Press ESC.

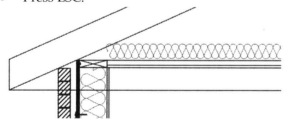

Creating the Roof Detail

- Offset the inclined line by 1". Next, close the end of the offset lines.

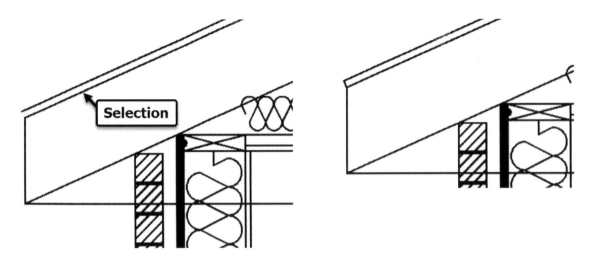

- Offset the new line by 0.5".
- Select the newly created offset line.
- Select **DASHED2** from the **Linetype** drop-down on the **Inspector** palette.
- Type **0.1** in the **Linetype Scale** box. Next, press ESC.

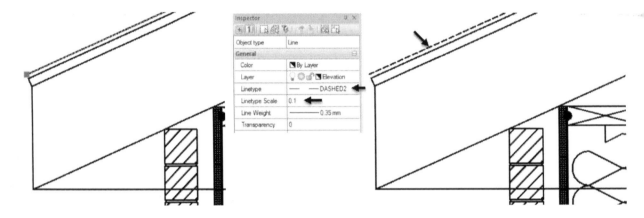

- Create another line with the offset distance of 0.75".

- Click **Modify > Lengthen objects** on the menu bar.
- Right-click and select the **DElta** option. Next, type 2.5 and press ENTER.
- Select the newly offset line.

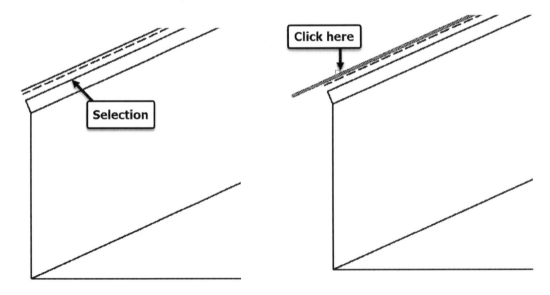

- Deactivate the **ORTHO** button on the status bar.
- On the menu bar, click **Tools > Coordinate System > Point and Angle**.
- Select the endpoint of the inclined line, as shown. Next, select a point of the inclined.

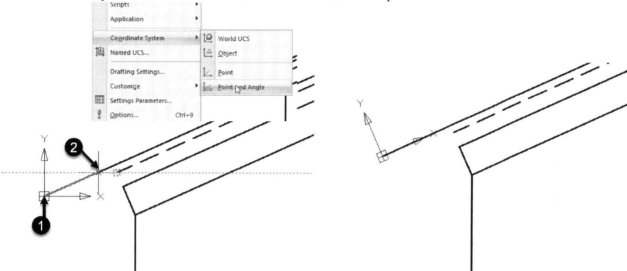

- Activate the **ORTHO** button on the status bar.
- Click the **Line** tool on the **Draw** toolbar.
- Select the endpoint of the inclined line, as shown. Next, move the pointer downward.
- Type 0.25 and press ENTER. Next, move the pointer toward the right.
- Type 0.375, and press ENTER.

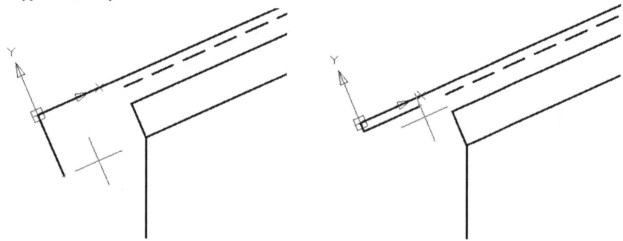

- On the menu bar, click **Tools > Coordinate System > World UCS**; the coordinate system is restored to its default location.

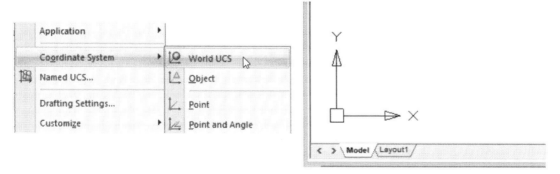

- Click the **Line** tool on the **Draw** toolbar. Next, select the endpoint of the last line.

- Move the pointer downward. Next, type 1.5 and press ENTER.
- Type @.375<225 in the command line and press ENTER.
- Press Esc.

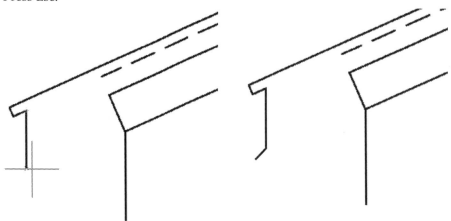

- On the **Draw** > **Arc** by > **Center, Start, Angle**. Next, select the midpoint of the line, as shown.
- Select the endpoint of the line, as shown. Next, type 180 and press ENTER.
- Delete the line between the endpoints of the arc.

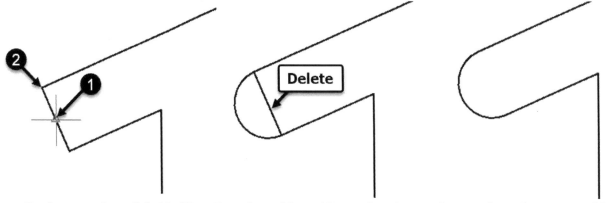

- On the menu bar, click **Modify** > **Lengthen objects**. Next, select the **Total** option from the command line.
- Type 9 and press ENTER. Next, click at the end portion of the inclined line, as shown.

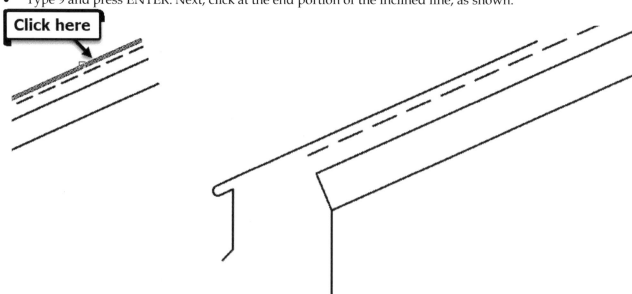

- Click **Draw** > **Rectangle by** > **Two points** on the menu bar.
- Select the corner point, as shown. Next, right-click and select the **Dimensions** option.
- Type 1 and press ENTER. Next, type 10 and press ENTER.

- Move the pointer downward and click to create a rectangle.

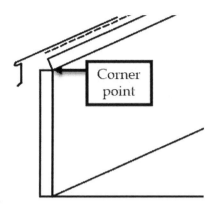

- Click **Draw > Rectangle by > Two points** on the menu bar.
- Select the top-left corner of the rectangle, as shown. Next, right-click and select the **Dimensions** option.
- Type 1 and press ENTER. Next, type 2.5 and press ENTER.
- Move the pointer downward and click to create a rectangle.

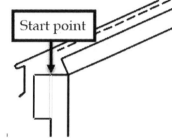

- Move the newly created rectangle downward by 0.5".

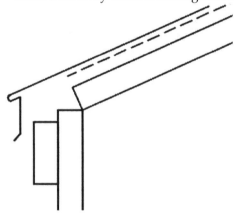

- Click the **Trim Vectors** icon on the **Modify** toolbar.
- Select the vertical edge of the brick, as shown. Next, press ENTER.
- Click on the horizontal line on the right side.

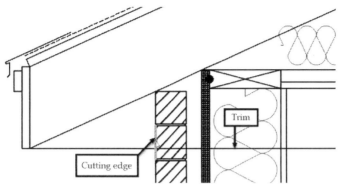

- Click the **Offset** tool on the **Modify** toolbar. Next, type 1, and press ENTER.
- Select the horizontal line trimmed in the last step.
- Move the pointer upward and click.
- Select the offset line. Next, move the pointer upward and click.

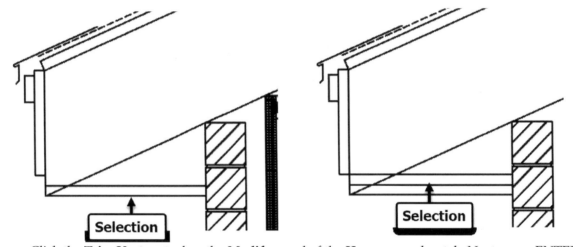

- Click the **Trim Vectors** tool on the **Modify** panel of the **Home** menu bar tab. Next, press ENTER.
- Select the portions of the lines, as shown.
- Select the **eRase** option from the command line and select the horizontal line. Next, press ENTER.

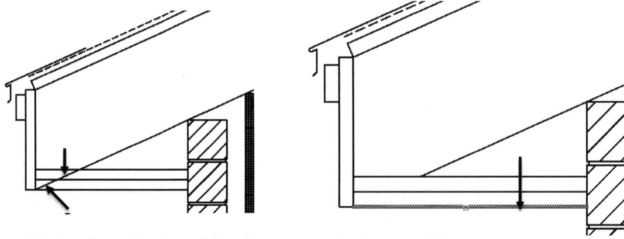

- Click the **Offset** tool on the **Modify** toolbar. Next, type 7 and press ENTER.
- Select the left vertical line of the veneer brick. Next, move the pointer toward the left and click.
- Press ENTER twice.
- Type 4 and press ENTER. Next, select the offset line.
- Move the pointer toward the left and click.

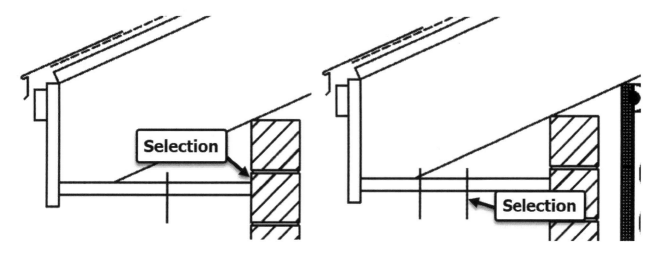

- Click the **Trim Vector** on the **Modify** toolbar. Next, select the portions of the lines, as shown.
- Create a line by selecting the corner points of the opening, as shown.

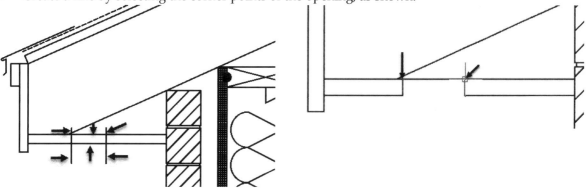

- Press ESC.
- Activate the **ORTHO** icon on the status bar.
- Select the newly created line and click **Scale** on the **Modify** toolbar.
- Select the midpoint. Next, move the pointer vertically downward.
- Type 1.25 as the scale factor, and then press ENTER.

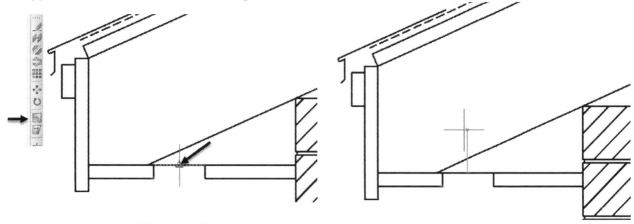

- Select the horizontal line and click on its midpoint grip.
- Move the pointer upward. Next, type 0.2 and press ENTER.
- Create an inclined line and pattern it, as shown.

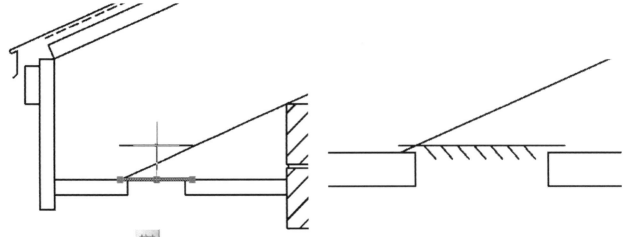

- Click the **Add Hatch** tool on the **Draw** toolbar.
- Select the **DASH** pattern from the **Pattern** drop-down.
- Type **90** and **2** in the **Angle** and **Scale** boxes, respectively.
- Click the **Add: Pick points** icon in the **Boundaries** section.
- Pick points in the areas, as shown. Next, press ENTER.

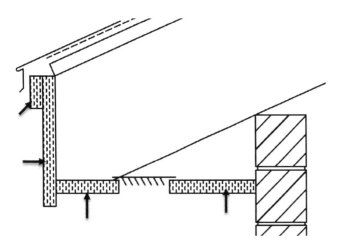

- On the menu bar, click **Draw > Rectangle by > Two Points**.
- Select the lower right corner of the rectangle, as shown. Next, right-click and select the **Dimensions** option.
- Type 6 and press ENTER.
- Type 5 and press ENTER. Next, move the pointer downward and click.

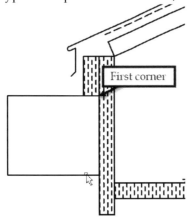

- Select the rectangle and click the **Move** tool on the **Modify** toolbar.
- Select the top right corner point of the rectangle.
- Move the pointer downward. Next, type 0.5, and press ENTER.
- Select the rectangle and click the **Move** tool on the **Modify** toolbar.
- Select the top right corner point of the rectangle.
- Move the pointer toward the left. Next, type 0.25, and press ENTER.

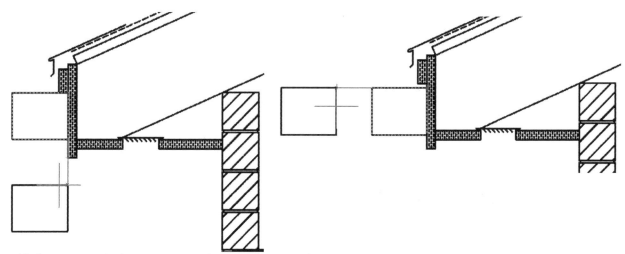

- Click **Draw** > **Circle** > **Center Radius** on the menu bar.
- Select the lower-left corner of the rectangle.
- Type 8 and press ENTER.
- Select the circle. Next, click on the centerpoint of the circle.
- Move the pointer toward the left. Next, type 7 and press ENTER.

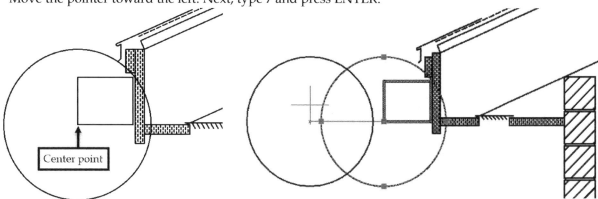

- Click the **Trim Vectors** on the **Modify** toolbar. Next, press ENTER.
- Trim the edges of the circle and rectangle, as shown.

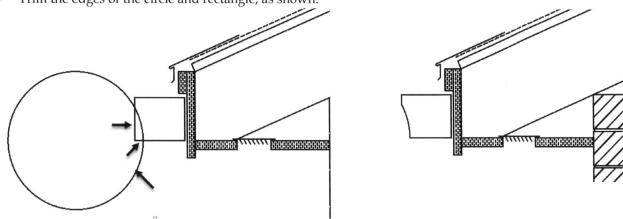

- Press ESC.

- Select the rectangle and click the **Explode** tool on the **Modify** toolbar.

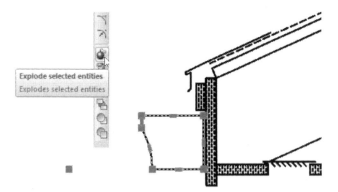

- Select the lines and arcs, as shown in the figure.
- Select the **0.70 mm** option from the **Line Weight** drop-down on the **Inspector** palette.

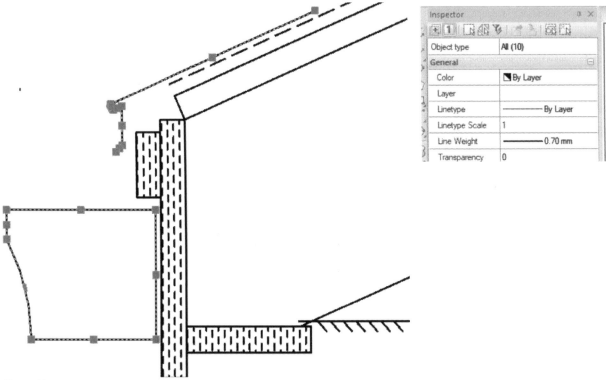

- Press Esc.
- Click the **Offset** tool on the **Modify** toolbar. Next, type 1.25 and press ENTER.
- Select the offset line, as shown in the figure. Next, move the pointer upward and click.

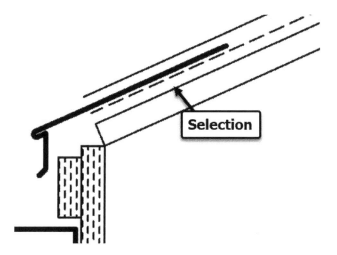

- Deactivate the **ORTHO** button on the status bar.
- On the menu bar, click **Tools > Coordinate System > Point and Angle**.
- Select the endpoint of the inclined line, as shown. Next, select a point of the inclined, and then press ENTER.

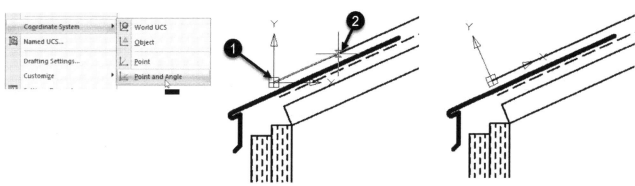

- Activate the **ORTHO** button on the status bar.
- Click the **Line** tool on the **Draw** toolbar.
- Select the endpoint of the offset line. Move the pointer upward.
- Type 2 and press ENTER.
- Type @7<355 in the command line and press ENTER.

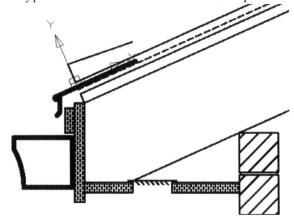

- Select the two newly created lines.
- Click the **2D Array** tool on the **Modify** panel.
- Select the **Rectangular Array** option from the **Array** dialog.
- Type 1 and 20 in the **Row** and **Column** boxes, respectively.
- Type 7 in the **Column Offset** box. Next, press ENTER.

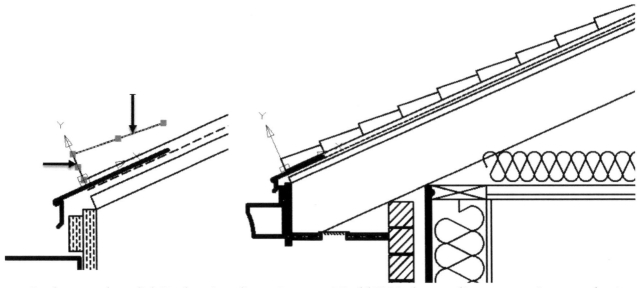

- On the menu bar, click **Tools > Coordinate System > World UCS**; the coordinate system is restored to its default location.

Adding Annotations
- On the menu bar, click **Format > Text Style**. Next, click the **Add New Style** icon on the top-right corner.
- Select the **Arial** font from the Font name drop-down. Next, type **2** in the **Height** box.

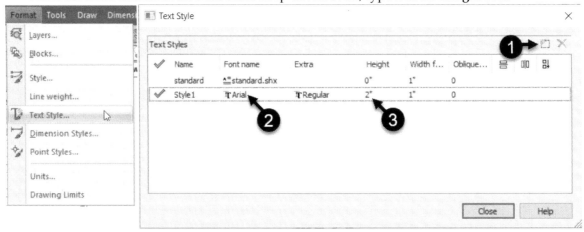

- Click **Close** on the **Text Style** dialog.
- Click **Tools > Settings Parameters** on the menu bar. Next, click the **Symbols** tab on the **Options** dialog.
- Expand the **Notes** branch and then expand the **Construction note** node.
- Specify the settings of the construction note, as shown.

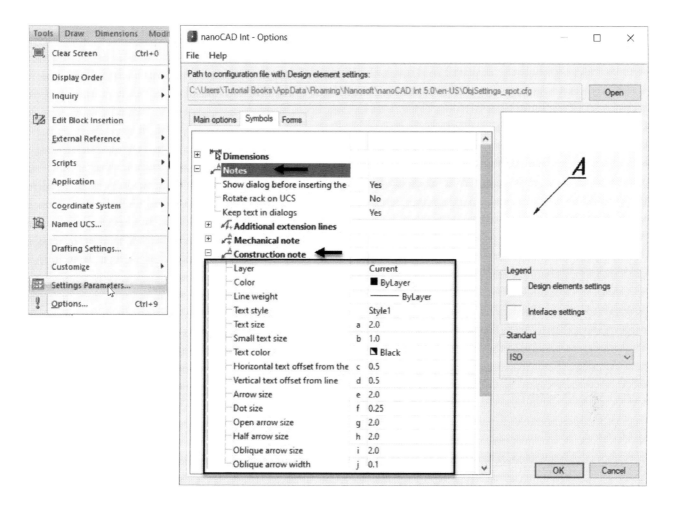

- Click **OK** on the **Options** dialog. Next, select the **Save to current document** option and click **OK**.
- Deactivate the **ORTHO** button on the status bar.
- On the menu bar, click **Draw > Notes > Position Notes**.
- Type **Insulation** and click **OK**.

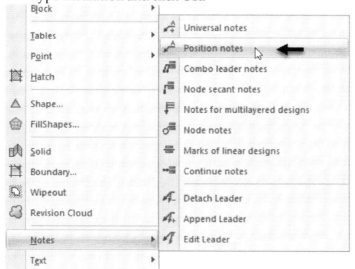

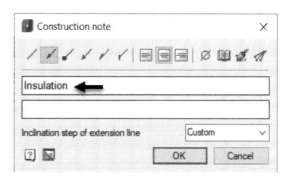

- Specify the start point of the leader on the insulation, as shown.
- Move the pointer diagonally toward the bottom right corner, and then click.

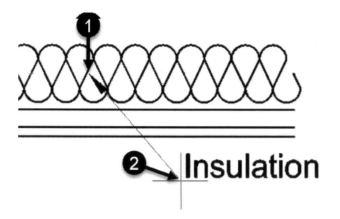

Insulation

- On the menu bar, click **Draw > Notes > Position Notes**.
- Type **Continuous Bead of Sealant** and click **OK**.
- Specify the start point of the leader on the circle, as shown.
- Move the pointer diagonally toward the bottom right corner, and then click.
- Click the **Properties Painter** tool on the **Properties** panel.

- Select the **Insulation** leader to specify the source object.
- Select the newly created leader; the properties of the source object are matched with the destination object.

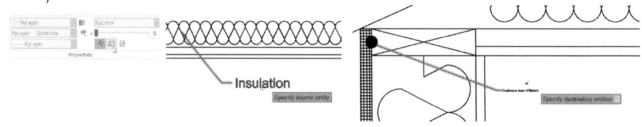

- Likewise, create the remaining leaders, as shown.

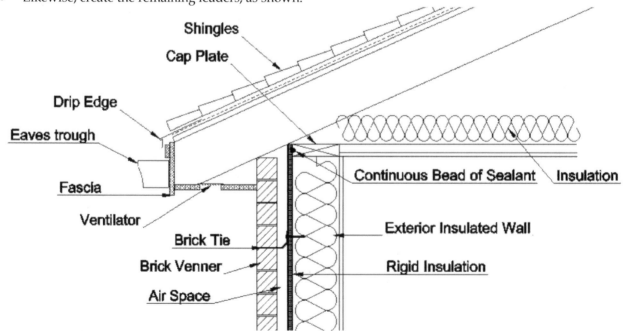

- Activate the **Ortho** button on the status bar.
- On the menu bar, click **Draw > Rectangle by > Two Points**.

- Click in the empty area. Next, right-click and select **Dimensions**.
- Type 6 and press ENTER. Next, type 12 and press ENTER. Next, click to create the rectangle.
- On the menu bar, click **Draw > Rectangle by > Two Points**.
- Select the top-right corner of the rectangle. Next, right-click and select **Dimensions**.
- Type 2 and press ENTER. Next, type 5 and press ENTER.
- Move the pointer downward and click.
- On the menu bar, click **Draw > Rectangle by > Two Points**.
- Select the bottom-left corner of the large rectangle. Next, right-click and select **Dimensions**.
- Type 2 and press ENTER. Next, type 5 and press ENTER.
- Move the pointer upward and click.

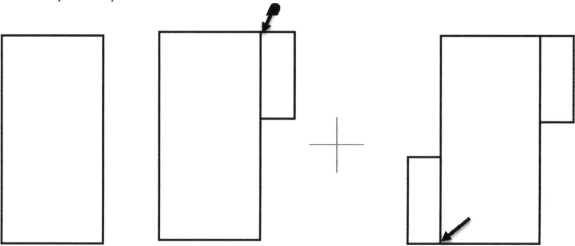

- Type L in the command line and press ENTER.
- Select the corner points of the rectangle in the sequence, as shown.

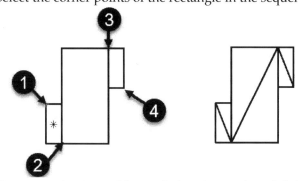

- Create two horizontal lines of 10 inches each and delete the rectangles.

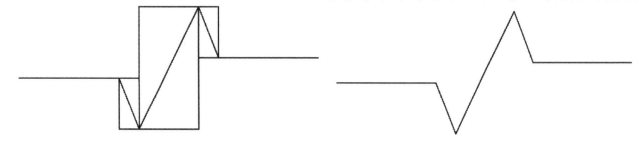

- Create a selection window across all the elements of the break line.
- Type CO and press ENTER. Next, select the point of the breakpoint, as shown.
- Move the pointer toward the wall detail and select the point, as shown. Next, press ESC.

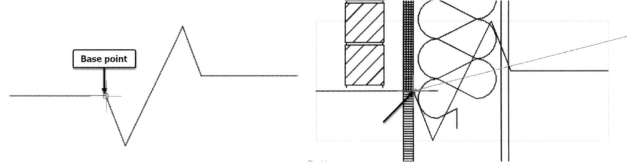

- On the menu bar tab, click **Trim Vectors** on the **Modify** toolbar.
- Select the elements of the break line and press ENTER.
- Trim the elements on the bottom side of the drawing.

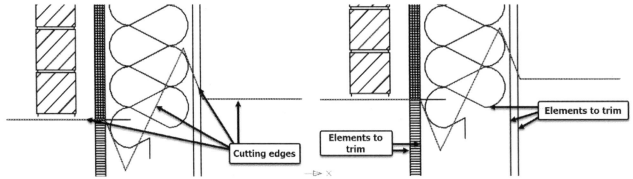

- Create the ANSI37 hatch by selecting the lines surrounding it.

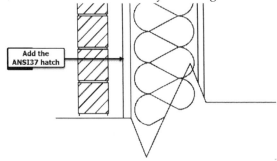

- Likewise, create the break lines and trim the elements, as shown.

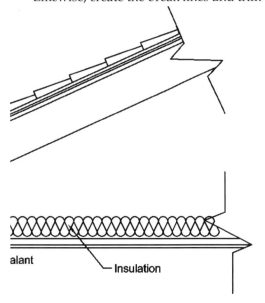

- Save and close the drawing file.

Tutorial 6: Sheets and Title Block

- Open the Tutorial 1 drawing file.

- Click the **Layout 1** tab at the bottom of the graphics window.

- Right click on the **Layout 1** tab and select **Page Setup**; the **Page Setup Manager** dialog appears. On the **Page Setup Manager** dialog, click the **New** button; the **New Plot Set** dialog appears.

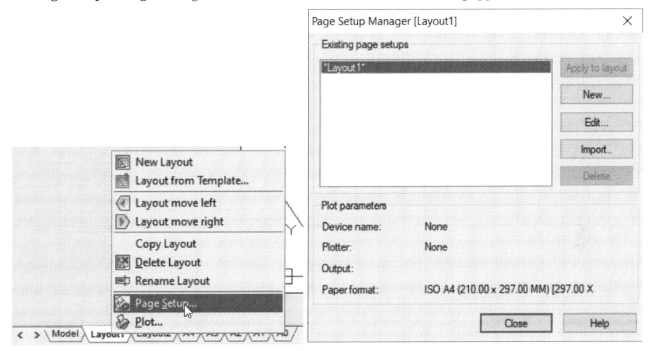

- Select the **Layout1** option from the **New Plot Set** dialog, and then click **OK**.

- On the **Page Setup** dialog, select **Adobe PDF** from the **Name** drop-down under the **Printer/plotter** group.

- Set the **Paper size** to **ARCH D**. Next, select the **Landscape** option.

- Set the **Scale** to **1'=1'**.

- Set the **Plot style table** to **monochrome.ctb**. Next, click **OK**.

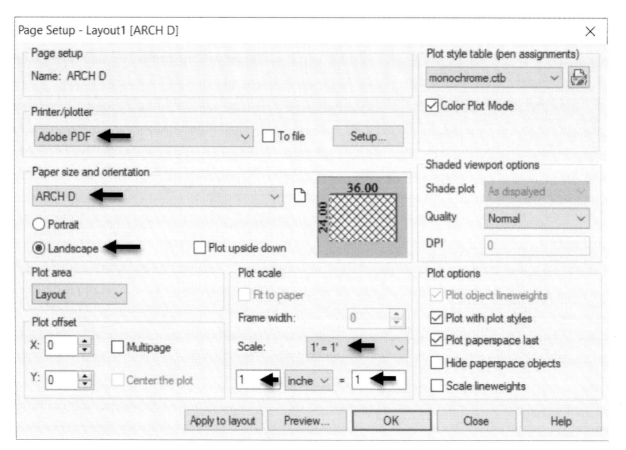

- Select the **ARCH D** page setup, and then click the **Apply to Layout** button.

- Click **Close** on the **Page Setup Manager** dialog.

- Right-click on the **Layout1** tab and select **Rename Layout**. Press ENTER to accept the Layout1.0

- Next, type **ARCH D** in the command line and press ENTER; the **Layout1** is renamed.

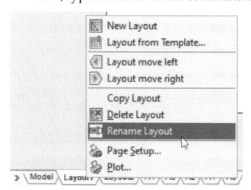

Creating the Title Block on the Layout

You can draw objects on layouts to create title blocks, borders, and viewports. However, it is not recommended to draw the actual drawing on layouts. You can also create dimensions on layouts.

- Click the **ARCH D** sheet tab.

- Create the **Title Block** layer and make it current.

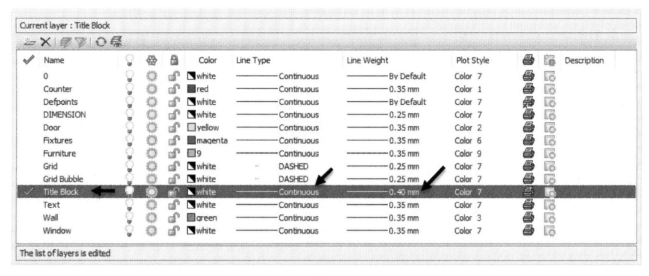

- Create the border and title block, as shown. Insert text inside the title block, as shown.

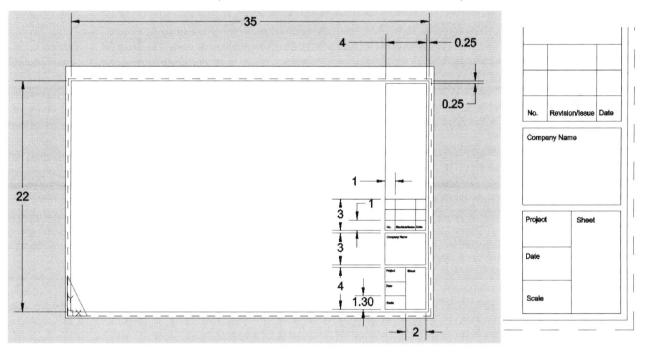

- On the menu bar, click **Draw > Block > Make**. Next, type **Title Block** in the **Name** box of the **Block Definition** dialog.

- Click the **Select objects** icon under the **Objects** section. Next, select the elements of the title block, and then press ENTER.

- Click the **Pick point** icon under the **Base point** section. Next, select the lower right corner point of the title block, and then press ENTER.

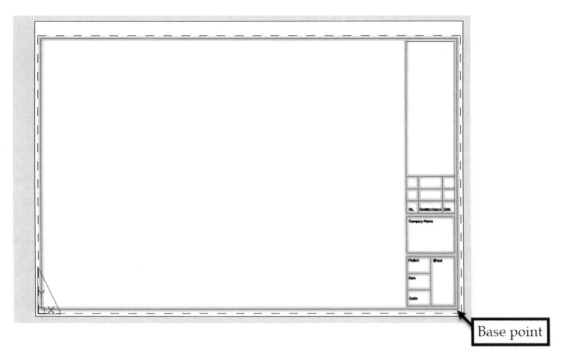

Base point

- Select the **Convert to block** option from the **Objects** section, and then click **OK**.

Creating Viewports in the Paper space

The viewports that exist in the paper space are called floating viewports because you can position them anywhere in the sheet and modify their shape size concerning the sheet.

- Open the **ARCH D** sheet, if not already open.
- Click **View > Viewports > Retangular** on the menu bar.
- Create the rectangular viewport by picking the first and second corner points, as shown in the figure.

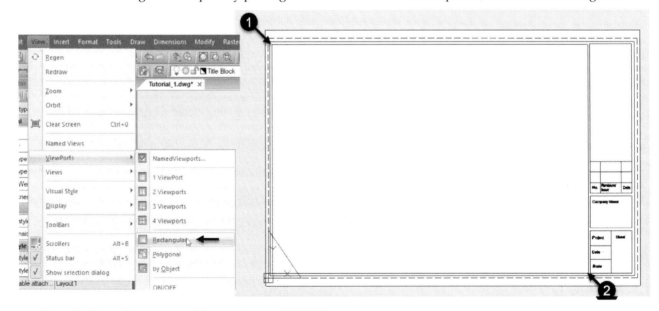

- Type 0.033 in the command line and press ENTER.
- Click inside the viewport; the model space inside the viewport is activated. Also, the viewport frame becomes thicker when you are in model space.

- Press and hold the left mouse button and drag the pointer toward the right.
- Double-click outside the viewport to lock it.

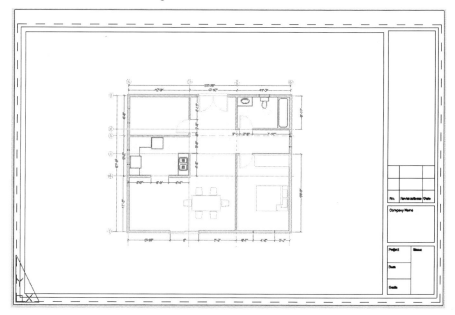

To hide viewport frames while plotting a drawing, follow the steps given below.

- Click the **Layer** icon on the **Properties** toolbar.

- In the **Layers** dialog, create a new layer called **Hide Viewports** and make it current.

- Deactivate the plotter symbol 🖶 under the **Plot** column of the **Hide Viewports** layer; this layer's object will not be print. Close the **Layers** dialog.

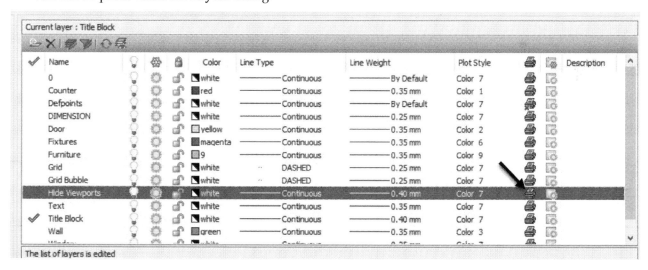

- Select the rectangular viewport in the **ARCH D** layout. Next, select the **Hide Viewports** layer from the **Layers** drop-down available on the **Properties** toolbar. The viewport frames are unplottable.

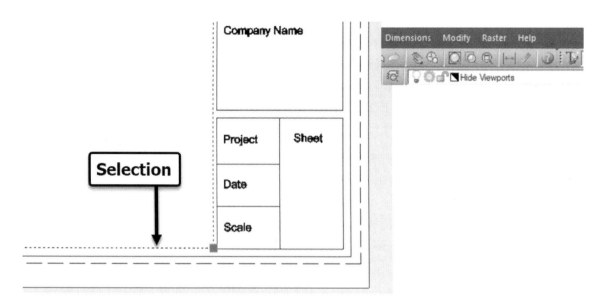

- Save the drawing file.

Tutorial 7: Plotting

- Open the Tutorial 1 file.

- On the menu bar, click **File > Plot**.

- Select the **monochrome.ctb** option from the **Print style table** section, and then click the **Edit** button.

- On the **Plot Style Table Editor** dialog, click the **Form view** tab.

- Select **Color 1** from the **Plot styles** list. Next, set the **Lineweight** to 0.1000 mm. Likewise, change the lineweights of the other colors, as shown.

Color	Lineweight
Color 1	0.1 mm
Color 2	0.2 mm
Color 3	1.0 mm
Color 4	0.5 mm
Color 5	0.7 mm
Color 6	0.5 mm
Color 8	0.09 mm
Color 9	0.05 mm

- Click **Save & Close** on the **Plot Style Table Editor** dialog.

- On the **Plot** dialog, click **Preview**; the print preview of the drawing appears.

- Click **Close** on the top right corner.

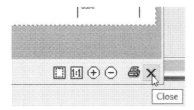

- Click **Plot** to plot the drawing. Next, specify the location and name of the PDF file.

- Click the **Save** button.

- Save and close the drawing.

Exercise

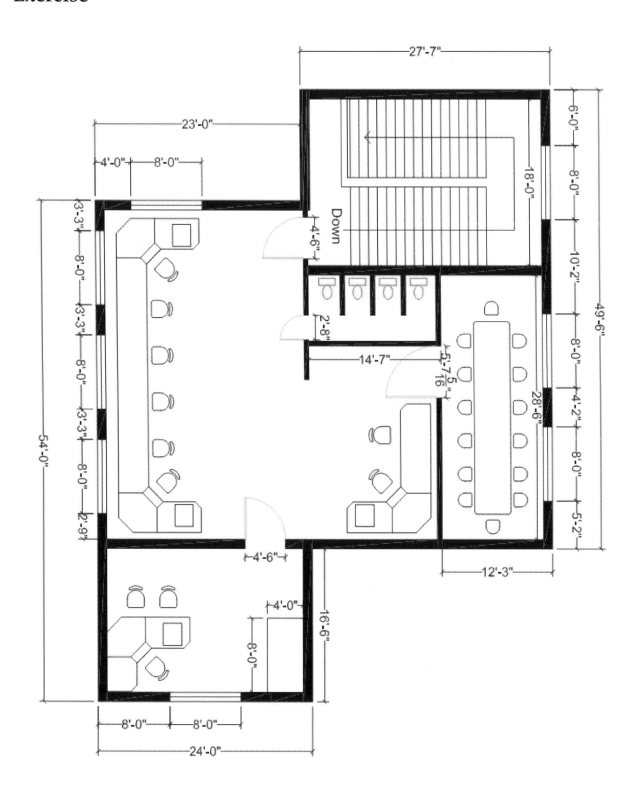

Made in the USA
Las Vegas, NV
29 November 2021

35591022R00094